SO-AHM-004

"Absorbing, perceptive portraits of people who are truly special . . . the author herself being one of them." —*Los Angeles Herald Examiner*

GOLDA MEIR—On being Prime Minister: "I had no particular relish for the job."

RUTH BELL GRAHAM—On interviews: "I feel a bit like someone doing a striptease when there's really not that much to show."

PRINCE CHARLES—On royalty: "The older I get, the more alone I become."

ANNE MORROW LINDBERGH—On the kidnapping: "It happens every night of my life."

MAO TSE-TUNG—On success: "Nothing is impossible if you dare to scale the heights."

MAMIE EISENHOWER—On her husband: "When Ike died, the light went out of my life."

"Shrewd, insightful, compassionate."
—Jessamyn West

"Subtle and affecting . . . when you lay down SPECIAL PEOPLE you feel you know better a half-dozen interesting people you may not have known before."
—*Library Journal*

SPECIAL PEOPLE

Julie Nixon Eisenhower

BALLANTINE BOOKS · NEW YORK

Copyright © 1977 by Julie Nixon Eisenhower

All rights reserved, including the right of reproduction in any form. Published in the United States by Ballantine Books, a division of Random House, Inc., New York, and simultaneously in Canada by Ballantine Books of Canada, Ltd., Toronto, Canada.

Library of Congress Catalog Card Number: 77-2129

ISBN 0-345-27530-6

This edition published by arrangement with Simon and Schuster, a Division of Gulf & Western Corporation

Manufactured in the United States of America

First Ballantine Books Edition: August 1978

Acknowledgments

In the summer of 1976 I found myself writing a book, which in itself—given the number of authors today—is not unusual. But in an office two doors away, also working on a book, was my father, who predicted after finishing his memoirs in 1961 that he would never undertake another similar project; and across the continent in Pennsylvania my father-in-law was immersed in his third book—the very two members of my family who had advised me not to subject myself to the self-imposed task of writing.

Though I had much I wanted to say in my book, that summer and fall I often found myself remembering their advice. Writing was not easy for me and it would have been far more difficult without the encouragement of many.

I am particularly grateful to Michael Korda, editor-in-chief of Simon and Schuster, for his enthusiasm for the project and for the editorial assistance he and his associates provided.

Acknowledgment

Two friends in Washington, Cynthia Milligan and Bruce Herschensohn, read each chapter as I wrote it and offered ideas and words of cheer. My spirits were lifted innumerable times also by transcontinental telephone calls from my lifelong friend Helene Drown of Los Angeles.

To Tricia, who let me use her apartment so often while I was writing the book, to my parents for their loving encouragement and constant support, and to David for his patience, help, and most of all his confidence that I could complete the job—heartfelt thanks.

And lastly, I want to express appreciation to all the Special People for generously sharing their time with me.

*For
my
family*

Contents

Contents

Introduction

In the spring of 1976, I walked from our apartment in Northwest Washington to the downtown shopping district, just a few blocks from the White House. I was not stopped once by anyone on the street. Nor, to my knowledge, was I recognized, something that had not happened since my father had become President in 1969. At that moment I realized a new period in my life had begun. David and I were no longer at the center. We could begin to pursue our lives with more freedom and objectivity than ever before. For the first time in a long time I felt like an observer.

I had frequently considered writing a book about my experiences during my father's years in public life, especially about some of the people I had met, many of them men and women who have shaped our lives, even shaped our world. I had observed some of them at close range and discovered that the image of the public person often did not reveal the inner, private person.

In *Special People* I describe six individuals who have affected my own thinking. Some have inspired me. Some have opened a new perspective to me. Others have taught me about love and patience. Each comes from a different world. Each represents a vastly different approach to life.

Golda Meir sacrificed her personal life to serve her ideal—the creation and preservation of Israel.

Ruth Graham has also lived for a cause. Her commitment has been to helping others develop their own faith in God.

Charles, Prince of Wales, was born to power. He is destined to exercise leadership in the future, a leadership which will be based on beliefs and values he has chosen to embrace despite the expectations and pressures of the publicists, courtiers and advisers who have surrounded him since birth.

Anne Morrow Lindbergh is a writer whose words have spoken directly to the concerns of millions—her perceptions have been shaped by a lifetime of public tragedy and success.

Mao was a revolutionary whose daring, intellect and tactical brilliance transformed China.

Mamie Eisenhower's existence has been one of complete devotion to her family. Her husband's credo, "Duty, Honor, Country," became her own.

In writing about these men and women, I explored questions which intrigued me. Above all, I learned that despite their diverse backgrounds, goals, and faiths, these six individuals share a passion: they love life. Life is an adventure, a challenge, to be lived to the fullest, to be made better for oneself and for others. Talking to these men and women and examining their lives helped me to learn more about my own life and attitudes. Perhaps in *Special People* the reader will find glimpses of himself and insights into his own life as well.

Golda Meir

"Don't become cynical. Don't give up hope. . . . There is idealism in this world. There is human brotherhood."

THE WOMAN WHO SAID, "I have no ambition to be somebody," is a legend already, great in her own lifetime—Golda *Shenayou* (our Golda). It is Israel, the dream and the state, that has given the world Golda Meir. For Israel's story is also her story.

Her eyes are full of pain and wisdom. But it is not unusual to see pain and the wisdom of many years in the eyes of a woman in her eighth decade. Nor is it surprising that those eyes are framed in deep smile lines. What was unexpected were the lightning changes from dark brooding to gentle concern.

And there was no fire in Golda Meir's eyes.

I had expected fire.

When Prime Minister Meir returned to her old elementary school in Milwaukee after more than sixty years, she told the children to get involved in "causes which are good for others, not only for yourselves." There has always been a cause for Golda. Her passionate belief in the concept of living for a cause or for duty has often made her a driven woman. But she has always been aware of the reasons for her struggles and her sacrifices. It is Israel's good fortune that the cause she embraced as a very young woman was that of a Jewish homeland.

She has seen her dream of a Jewish state come true, although Israel is still not accepted by her Arab neighbors, and year after year Golda Meir's hopes of establishing a lasting peace have remained only that— hopes. Yet she does not give up. She has a cause and nothing can discourage her, neither chronic incapacitating migraines nor phlebitis, neither disappointment in people nor in nations, neither military disasters nor political defeat.

How is it that this woman who had "no ambition to be somebody" achieved greatness and power?

I visited Mrs. Meir in her temporary retirement office in Ramat Aviv, a fairly new area in the outskirts of Tel Aviv where few trees or shrubs soften the desert bleakness. She works in an austere two-room suite, just her office and a small anteroom staffed by one secretary, in an equally austere and utilitarian gray government building. I was struck by the grim ruggedness of the land as I drove out from Tel Aviv. In many ways Golda Meir is like this land. She is rough-hewn and solid, a presence. For years she has clung tenaciously to these rocks, this sand. And, like rock and sand, she can be undeniably forbidding.

She is known and loved for her warm-heartedness, but as we talked I began to understand all the stories of how her colleagues in the government approached their initial meetings with Mrs. Meir with as much fearful apprehension as eagerness. When I asked a question she did not like or broached a subject that she did not want to comment on, she became absolutely rock-like. She did not move her stocky body. She did not respond. She seemed rooted to her chair. Immobile. Silent. Her eyes cold and dark. If she chose to answer, she spoke briefly and there was finality in her voice, even an edge of severity. One could not pursue the question or the subject further. I became very aware that I was talking to a woman who had had to make many difficult decisions, and whose voice and views could never be dismissed.

Her appearance is as forbidding as her manner. Her hair is pulled back and shaped into a flat bun. No longer thick, it lies close to her head. Unnoticeable. She has worn her hair long all her life because her husband loved it that way. And so does her son. It has never been washed at a beauty parlor. Golda claims they cannot get it clean enough. Even when she was Prime Minister, she would often end her long days by washing her hair at two or three in the morning.

She wears no makeup. She came to this arid land as a young woman to work with her hands, to build a new land. Nothing so trivolous as makeup could be considered, and as the years of struggle succeeded each other, there was never time nor heart for Golda to consider her appearance or her clothes. Characteristically, when she flew to America in 1947 in a frantic, last-minute appeal for arms to protect Israel from Arab attack, she thought nothing of boarding the plane with no luggage other than her handbag. And as Prime Minister, she never seemed to give a second thought to climbing a ladder to an observation post, her unwieldy body and utilitarian underwear in view of the soldiers and officials clustered below.

The physical punishment of her life's work—the one-hundred-and-one-hour hunger strike she led when she was forty-eight years old to protest the British refusal to allow refugees to land in Palestine, for example, and the sixteen-hour days she works even now —all this has left its mark. Her legs are thick and swollen, encased in heavy gray support hose. She suffers from a circulatory condition which has been aggravated by her refusal to spare herself as well as by two injuries incurred during the course of duty: fragments from a bomb that exploded at a cabinet meeting lodged in her leg and had to be cut out; and on a fund-raising mission in New York City her leg was broken in a taxi accident. She now walks slowly and heavily. But her arms and hands are still strong and vital. Her hands are worn, a reminder of the hundreds of holes she dug in the hostile rocky land to plant trees when she lived in the kibbutz, of the desperately poor years in Jerusalem in the 1930s when she took in laundry to pay for her children's schooling, and of the dozens of coffee cups and plates she still washes every day. But as she gestured, I noticed a coat of clear polish on the short, neatly filed nails, a reminder that the pioneer and the former Prime Minister is also a woman.

I felt quite awed by her, but there were many moments during our talk when Mrs. Meir was even warmer and more caring than I had expected. Her first words to me, even before she had shown me into her office, had been "How is your dear mother?" And as she sat down, she pressed for more details on my mother's health. "But tell me more," she said with sincere concern. Several times during the course of the morning, she told me that she wished she had been able to ask me to her apartment instead of the office, as if apologizing that the small cakes and nuts which accompanied our coffee and the two bouquets of pink sweetheart roses could not make up for the intimacy of her own home.

The night I arrived in Israel, I had driven from my hotel in Tel Aviv to Ramat Aviv to look at the building where Golda lives. Just a three-minute drive from her office, it is a drab, two-story apartment complex, resembling nothing so much as a squat concrete box. When she was Prime Minister, Golda had said, "I know about low wages. I live among the working people." She still lives among the working people. They are her friends and neighbors. But her experiences set her apart even from them. Golda's apartment was immediately identifiable, for instance, because of the sentry box outside. As a former Prime Minister, she is still guarded. Five or six packing boxes literally filled up her tiny yard. She was in the process of having her apartment painted, which was why our meeting took place in her office.

The office itself was unexpectedly impersonal. I had formed a mental picture of it beforehand. There would be her desk crowded with papers and memorabilia, a comfortable sofa and an easy chair, bookshelves crammed with books and photographs of family and colleagues on every surface. Just a week before, I had visited Clara Stern, Golda's younger sister who lives in Bridgeport, Connecticut, and Clara had told me of the fierce love and respect her sister had for books. Every once in a while Golda asks Clara to help her weed through the memorabilia that every public person seems to collect, but whenever Clara suggests that her sister get rid of a book, Golda is horror-struck. Even an out-dated tome of statistics is held on to and treasured.

But there were no books evident in the office. It looked like a motel room, and the stiff little bouquets of sweetheart roses only accentuated the look. The furniture, completely nondescript, consisted of a coffee table in front of a small sofa flanked by the two chairs in which we sat, and, of course, her desk and desk chair. It was an anonymous room.

As we drank our coffee, I told Mrs. Meir about my visit to Israel ten years before with my parents and sister. Since none of us had ever been to Israel, Tel Aviv was the highlight of our family vacation through Europe that summer. We had been in the city for only two hours when an invitation came to visit David Ben-Gurion, the man who had led the fight to found the State of Israel, at his small house on the outskirts of the city. Tricia and I were rarely included in my parents' invitations, but this time we were, probably because in 1959 Ben-Gurion had visited our home while on an official trip to Washington, Tricia, then in the seventh grade, was studying Judaism in school and my parents arranged for her to meet him. She had a test the next morning and Ben-Gurion, with great patience, answered some of her questions, explaining the significance of the menorah and why the Jewish holy day is Saturday instead of Sunday. Tricia was excited to meet the country's first Prime Minister— and she got an "A" on her exam.

When we arrived at Ben-Gurion's home we went immediately upstairs to his tiny study. All four walls were solidly lined with books so that the room seemed even smaller. While my father and Ben-Gurion were talking, his wife took Tricia and me aside and told us how difficult it had been—she described it as "an ordeal"—to convince her husband, who had insisted his salary as Prime Minister be no higher than that of the average working man, that their children should have the luxury of music lessons. I asked if her husband played any instruments and Mrs. Ben-Gurion had answered, "No, he just plays on my nerves."

When Golda heard the story, her face lit up and she laughed, a low pleasant laugh. A smile lingered on her face. And at that moment I glimpsed beauty. Her smile is surprisingly sweet and it changes the expression in her eyes to a gentle softness. I had seen the same expression in an extraordinary photograph of Golda her sister had shown me the previous week. It was her favorite picture of Golda, Clara told me, and I could understand why. When Golda's eyes take on that softness, she is a beautiful woman.

But now, the smile faded. Her eyes suddenly became somber and all-knowing again. She was quiet. Perhaps thinking of the past. Of Ben-Gurion.

"He was a loner," she said slowly. "When he was not at work with people, he was always writing, writing, writing. He was one of the greatest men, not only in Israel, but in the world."

"What makes a great man?" I asked her.

Without hesitating, she replied, "You have to have an ideal. There is a difference between someone who has great financial success or great academic success and a great man. The great men gave their lives to an ideal which everyone thought was crazy—and which became a reality."

As she spoke, the "great men" suddenly became those men and women she had watched create a new country. The pioneering men and women who had come to this desolate land of sand and stones and

8

scorching sun and slowly, painfully, had made the desert flower and had built a Jewish state.

"They were largely self-made individuals," she said, "who achieved much with very little. They had great minds and a lot of knowledge, some of which they acquired by themselves."

After a pause, she added, "And they had moral quality. This enabled them to influence even the young."

It was a revealing, if unintentional, self-portrait. Golda had known few advantages as a child, but she had had ideals and dreams. The ideal of becoming a teacher. Despite her parents' objections (they wanted her to stop school after the eighth grade and go to work), she insisted on acquiring an education. And she had had that other ideal, that daring dream, "which everyone thought was crazy," of a homeland for the Jews.

Golda has that moral quality which enables her to influence "even the young" even now, even as a woman in her seventies. She has never been too busy to talk with young people. A typical Golda story is of the time during her first year as Prime Minister when she learned that a group of American students at the Hebrew University in Jerusalem, who were unhappy over her statements supporting the United States involvement in Vietnam, were planning a protest demonstration. She made a point of squeezing time out at the end of a busy day to meet with them in her official residence. The students talked with Golda for two hours. They ate her cake and drank her coffee. When she had to leave for an appointment, she invited them to stay on and watch television.

Ideals, determination, intelligence, character, the ability to influence the young—Golda has all the qualities of greatness that she had singled out for me. Her greatest strength of all, according to one of her oldest friends, may be her utter honesty about herself and about situations. Others have been impressed by the same quality.

When the Labor Party elected Golda as their nominee for Prime Minister in 1969, Moshe Dayan abstained from voting because he did not feel she was the best person for the job. But Golda won his respect almost immediately because she was "straightforward and direct." He found that "she did not resort to evasion."

It was Golda's clear perception of the world and the place of weak peoples or nations in it that made her dedicate her entire being to Jewish statehood. I asked her about the 1938 International Conference on Refugees which was called by Franklin D. Roosevelt at Evian-les-Bains, France, to discuss what to do with the Jews and other refugees fleeing from Hitler's Germany. Palestine was not even given full representation at the conference and so Golda was in the audience as "the Jewish observer from Palestine." Sitting in the midst of the luxury and beauty of the Hotel Royal overlooking Lake Geneva, Golda found it a searing experience to listen to the representatives of thirty-two countries say that they would like to take in substantial numbers of refugees but were unable to do so because it would be too great an economic burden. The conference was a turning point in Golda Meir's life.

"I realized then," she told me, "that a world which is not necessarily anti-Semitic—because Hitler was denounced at the conference and there was considerable pro-Jewish sentiment—could stand by and see others who were weaker victimized." Mrs. Meir, an old, gray woman now in a plain blue shirtdress, spoke without bitterness, but her voice was heavy and lifeless.

"We can't depend on any others," she said flatly. And there was a long pause. At that conference in 1938, Golda did not know what lay ahead in the Holocaust. How could she have conceived of the extermination of six million Jews? Or dreamed that one day she would listen to a Nazi Commandant testify at

Adolf Eichmann's trial that "very frequently women would hide their children under their clothes, but of course, when we found them we would send the children in to be exterminated"?

Finally Golda said, "I remember at the end of that conference I said to the press—'I hope I live to see the day when Jews won't be pitied.' Today people are for us. People are against us. But no one pities us."

She has lived to see the day. The Jews may still be the object of hatred, but with their highly trained and disciplined army, they are not to be pitied.

I asked Mrs. Meir if, now that she is removed from the turmoil of being at the center of government, she has any greater understanding of the hatred that threatens Israel's survival. She replied, "The Arabs are not against Jews. They are against Israelis. And as for those who support the Palestinian terrorists," she shook her head and then went on, "in order to justify supporting terrorists, you must picture the object of your hate as something very terrible." Her knowledge of the Arabs' irrational fear of "something very terrible" is what compels Golda to be so adamant about Israel's need to be strong.

There was another question that I had to ask Golda Meir. But before I spoke, I could not help but think of the scorching sun outside and the sandy soil surrounding the concrete of her office building, of this inhospitable strip of land—only 8,000 square miles, not as large as our State of Maryland—that the Israelis have clung to and cultivated and slowly transformed into a modern nation. I asked my question.

"Mrs. Meir, fifty years from now will Israel still be in a virtual state of siege? When will peace come?"

"Peace depends upon two things," she answered without hesitation. "It depends on the Arabs and it depends on the world. But the world is giving in to terrorism. It is giving in to oil."

I reacted to this by describing the inability of the United Nations to counter the wave of terrorism as "a joke." But before I could finish my thought, Mrs. Meir interrupted me.

"A joke?" She spat the words out.

"It is a tragedy. Not a joke. The U.N. is a tragedy. There sits the world. The Arabs, the Moslems and the Communist bloc rule the world. They can pass anything they want to. And what shocks me most is that the free world just abstains."

She spoke bluntly of the lack of courage and moral conviction of the nations who abstain rather than protest each terrorist outrage. Her voice was low and dispassionate. She spoke slowly, so slowly that I could write her words down in longhand. But there was a look of disgust and frustration on her face. She could control her emotions when she talked of the reality of oil ruling the world, but that did not mean that her anger that the socialist nations of Europe had failed to support Israel, the only socialist democracy in the Middle East, had diminished or disappeared. The hearts of these nations may be with Israel, but their pragmatic heads are with the Arabs—they import three-fourths of their oil from the Middle East. As a lifelong idealist, Golda Meir finds their pragmatism a bitter pill to swallow.

She is also angry and outraged at the uses the Arabs put their oil revenues to—"All that money on the arms race!" she exclaimed. And she told me, indignant at the senselessness of it, that the infant mortality rate in the Arab countries is the highest in the world.

Golda, who has four grandsons and a granddaughter, has both a world leader's and a woman's very personal interest in peace. Her eldest grandson has just entered the Army and the other three will follow soon; her granddaughter has already done her Army service. She is extremely proud of her grandchildren. Her voice becomes mellow and happy when she talks about them. And like any grandmother, she loves to talk about them.

With pride she told me that her youngest grandson

was asked once how it felt to have a famous relative. "Well," he replied, "I tried to keep it a secret, but it leaked."

Her nineteen-year-old grandson who is in the Army is also having his difficulties keeping it quiet that his grandmother is the former Prime Minister. When he learned that his grandmother was going to visit his base, he telephoned her and begged, "Please, don't come." She canceled her visit. A few days later, he had an even closer call. With glee, Golda re-created the scene for me. Her grandson and some of his Army buddies were discussing fellow soldiers on the base. They had discovered that the son of the Ambassador to the United Nations and the son of the head of the Air Force as well as sons of other prominent government officials were in their company. And, rumor had it, so was Golda Meir's grandson. At this point, Mrs. Meir acted out the incident. "There he was. Sitting and shivering," she said with a smile. And she hunched her shoulders, pulled her elbows in and brought her arms close to her chest as she rubbed her hands in mock fright. "He was saved only because many are named Meir."

As Golda talked about her beloved grandchildren, she said—and it was obvious this was something that she and her family had often discussed—"We figured it out that for the next ten or twelve years the boys will be in the Army. There will be two at a time, all the time. Perhaps as many as three." Almost as an after-thought, she told me something her son Menachem had said only a few weeks before. " 'Mother, when I was a child, you never would buy me a play gun or any military toys—and yet I've lived with guns all my life.' " I could almost hear Golda ticking off the conflicts in her mind—World War II, the struggle for statehood when Menachem was a member of the Haganah (the under-ground Jewish self-defense organization), and the three wars since

Independence: Suez, the Six-Day War, the Yom-Kippur War.

When one considers the anguish of watching and waiting that will be hers, the terrifying likelihood that one or all of her grandsons might be killed the next time war breaks out, it is difficult to question Mrs. Meir's call for a strong Israel. But her belief in that necessity goes deeper than love of family. It has to do with an elemental human right, the right to exist. Mrs. Meir belongs to that older generation who actually watched the survivors of the Holocaust land on the beaches of Israel. She can never forget that one million children—a whole generation—were annihilated.

Golda Meir is old. Older than her years. And she is weary. More weary than she likes to admit. During most of our conversation, she kept her body still as if glad of the chance to sit quietly. She did not gesture often. And she spoke slowly and tiredly. When she first sat down she took her butane lighter and white leatherette cigarette case out of her pocketbook so that they would be within easy reach on the coffee table. I knew that she was a chain-smoker, and I had heard the story of the most recent excuse she had given her doctor for not quitting. "At my age," she had asked, "what other pleasures do I have in life?" But while I was there, she smoked only occasionally. Almost as if the effort of lighting the cigarette was too much.

We spoke briefly of the plans to do a Broadway play based on her life and the possibility that she might come to New York for the premiere. "If I'm still around, I'll see it," she said, and went on to add that she can no longer stand the pace of a trip jammed with events and people as she has in the past.

"It's not just the events," she said heavily. "It's in between the events. It takes everything out of me." And, indeed, the major concession that Golda has made to old age is to cut down on her customary schedule of back to-back visitors to seeing just four or five people or groups a day.

Golda is not only physically weary, but also she is weary of the endless interviews, the same questions over and over. She refuses to discuss personal matters, to answer questions about her marriage or to comment on her family's support or lack of support for her career. And now that she is no longer in government, she cannot, as she has for decades, fill her conversation with her views on the issues facing Israel and how they should be resolved. So there are silences. Her reluctance to discuss political matters indicated that she still wields a great deal of power. She scrupulously tries to refrain from commenting on the sensitive issues facing the two major political parties. It may be that my impression of her bone-deep weariness came in part from her inability to talk spiritedly and with purpose about actions and decisions that will affect the daily lives of Israelis. The role of elder stateswoman comes hard to this activist who has devoted her life to government.

Despite her weariness, however, and despite her non-official status, she maintains a pace that is only slightly less hectic than before her retirement. She continues to push herself to the edge of endurance, although she admits that quick retreats to the bathroom to splash cold water on her face no longer revive her as effectively as they did in the past. As she described her previous day's activities to me, she said, "It was a very big day. I was really dead tired."

She had given two television interviews the day before we met—one French, one American—discussing the impasse in Arab-Israeli negotiations. She had had several appointments with people in and out of government and dealt with the day's share of the five hundred or so letters she receives each week. She had gone to bed at ten. At eleven there was a telephone call from Washington, from the Israeli Ambassador to the United States, her old friend Simcha Dinitz. He told her the American interview would be shown in the United States later in the evening. Golda thanked him and went back to sleep. At one o'clock the Ambassador called again. The telecast had gone well.

Dinitz was Mrs. Meir's political aide when she was Prime Minister and they had a close relationship. He was the man who day after day had read all the cables to her. "Golda learns by listening," he told me. He knows her love of being at the center of things, in pace with events. And so the night he telephoned, he knew that no matter how late it was, Golda would want to know how things had gone. And besides, he knew she would fall back to sleep without any trouble. She herself told me that her ability to fall asleep anywhere at any time is "my strongest point."

Over the years she has trained herself to get along with no more than four hours of sleep a night for several days at a time. But at the end of a stretch of twenty-hour days, she simply collapses and will sleep for fourteen hours without waking. Her sister told me that one of their mother's greatest problems with "Goldie" used to be trying to get her to go to bed at night—and then trying to get her up again in the morning.

During the War of Attrition in 1971 and 1972, when the Arabs waged an undeclared war of sporadic nighttime attacks along the border, Golda left orders to be awakened each time an Israeli was killed. Clara was staying with her sister at the time and she told me, "The phone would ring all night long." And Golda's ability to fall asleep easily deserted her during those long nights. The tension was relieved only once. The phone rang at three in the morning. Golda picked it up and listened as the operator said, "I want to report that twenty-six sheep were killed."

The Prime Minister had ordered that she be told about all casualties, but *sheep?* She turned over and tried to go back to sleep.

Within a few minutes the phone rang again. "I'm

16

sorry, Mrs. Meir," the operator apologized, "it was only twenty-five."

The story made me realize just how intense a leader Golda was, always deeply involved in every aspect of her job. She insisted on knowing exactly what was going on and when and where. "I never, never signed a letter as Prime Minister," she told me, "without reading it first. No matter who had prepared it for me." This kind of meticulous attention to detail meant that she constantly drove herself to her emotional and physical limits.

And her insistence that she be informed of every casualty testifies to her great heart and conscience. To her, each death was a personal loss. Golda is a truly rare woman, a woman of steel—and heart. The adversity and pain of her early years explain a great deal about why she is that kind of woman. And yet, when one understands what she has been through, it seems remarkable that she drew courage and strength from adversity and pain, rather than bitterness.

Ben-Gurion has been quoted as saying that Golda "had a difficult childhood," but difficult is much too mild a word to describe Golda's life as a daughter of a poor Jewish carpenter in Russia at the turn of the century. It is hard to imagine the poverty of such a childhood. Four brothers and a sister died in infancy from disease caused by poor living conditions and malnutrition. Golda remembers always being hungry as a child. Her sister Sheyna, nine years older, occasionally fainted from hunger at school. But even worse than hunger was being different. Being despised because she and her family were Jewish. One of Golda's first memories, when she was a little over three, was of her father barricading the entrance of their home in Kiev with wooden planks because of the fear of a pogrom. Her father took down the planks the next day—the attack did not come—but Golda could not forget that people filled with hate against the "Christ-killers" might surge through the streets, brandishing clubs any day in the future.

It was Sheyna who gave meaning to Golda's consciousness of being different. She made Golda proud to be a Jew. Sheyna, whom Golda says was the greatest influence on her life apart from her husband, was a Zionist, and Zionists believed that Jews not only had a right to exist, but also had an historic mission as well—to return to Zion and establish a land of their own. And Golda accepted this mission. When she was seventeen, Golda decided that she must live and work in Palestine, not just talk about it. It was a courageous decision. Palestine was still an uncharted frontier. It would be another two years before the British government announced that it favored the establishment of "a national home for the Jewish people" there.

In her memoirs, Golda wrote of Sheyna: "I think of her constantly." I asked why Sheyna had had such an influence on her. "Was it that she was an idealist?" I ventured.

For a moment, she looked offended. And then, her voice incredulous, she repeated "An idealist?" as if questioning how it was possible I did not recognize instantly the extraordinary strength and courage of her older sister. "An idealist," she responded, "and strong!" she added with great emphasis. When I had asked Clara earlier to describe Sheyna, her first words —without the slightest hesitation—were, "She had lots of guts."

Golda went on to talk about Sheyna. With admiration in her eyes, she said, "Sheyna wouldn't budge left or right from her ideals." In 1903, just before her father emigrated to America, he moved the family to Pinsk. But in Pinsk, Sheyna, despite her mother's objections, became deeply involved with the forbidden Socialist-Zionist movement. The possible consequences of Sheyna's activities—torture, imprisonment—so terrified her mother that she was forced to take her three daughters (Clara was born in 1902) to America before her husband was earning enough money to support them adequately. In 1906, they made the long journey from Russia to the United States.

Golda Meir has written movingly of her conflicts with her family once they were settled in Milwaukee over her desire to make something of her life. Her sister Clara feels strongly that those who have read only Mrs. Meir's autobiography cannot have a full understanding of why their parents opposed Golda so often. Clara said, "My father was a really wonderful person but he simply was not successful." And so her mother's obsession was only the natural wish that her daughters marry "good providers," men who could spare them the poverty and, most of all, the terrifying insecurity which she had endured. That is why she simply could not tolerate the idea of her daughter signing a teacher's contract which forbade marriage. She wanted Golda to drop out of high school and go to work. At fifteen, Golda turned her back temporarily on her parents and fled to Denver to join Sheyna, who had gone there to recover from tuberculosis. In Denver, Golda Mabovitch met Morris Meyerson, a quiet young man whose parents, like hers, were immigrants. She disappointed her parents again by marrying him on the eve of her nineteenth birthday.

Morris Meyerson gave Golda "so much I did not get from my home," an appreciation for art and music and literature. And a new kind of love, gentle and understanding. He was a man of unusual sensitivity. And yet the marriage eventually became a source of frustration, pain and conflict for Golda and Morris. Mrs. Meir (she took a Hebrew name at Ben-Gurion's insistence when she became a member of his cabinet) is a woman who, when faced with unfavorable odds or even the near-certainty of failure, always defied the odds and fought. But her marriage was one situation she could not salvage. It was not something she could deal with simply by gritting her teeth and fighting on.

Golda married Morris with the understanding that they would emigrate to Palestine, and he kept his promise, even though as Clara was to tell me so many years later, "Morris was never cut out to be a pioneer." He loved music and art. Palestine was a desert wasteland, where only the sturdiest of pioneers could survive.

At Merhavia, the kibbutz where they settled, the heat, the periodic infestations of flies, and the never-ending bouts of malaria reduced Morris to near-chronic illness. They left the kibbutz and moved to Jerusalem. It was not solely Morris' health that prompted the move. There was another very important reason. They both wanted a child. Morris was opposed to the collective child-rearing of the kibbutz. Golda wrote, "He refused to have children at all unless we left." The following November, their son Menachem was born in Jerusalem.

Golda had grown up in an environment in which the good daughter was the girl who grew up to be a good mother, but the four years in Jerusalem when Golda, at Morris' urging, tried to be a full-time mother and homemaker were the most miserable of her life. She had come to Palestine to help build a just and progressive society for the Jews and there were many times when she doubted, possibly even hated, herself for not being satisfied with less. When she was thirty, she talked of the anguish of the modern woman and posed a question for all working women—and most of all herself— "Is there something wrong with me if my children don't fill up my life?"

During those years in Jerusalem when her son and, two years later, her daughter Sarah were born, Golda and Morris experienced fearful poverty and hunger like the hunger she remembered as a child in Pinsk. The thought of her children going hungry was agony. She wrote Sheyna about her despair when she was refused bread and margarine on credit. And in 1928, Golda the idealist, the woman with a cause, the activist, seized the opportunity to become secretary of the Women's Labor Council of the Histadrut (the General Federation of Jewish Labor). It meant that she had to move to Tel Aviv. She found an apartment in Tel Aviv for herself and the children. Morris stayed in Jerusalem and visited them on weekends. This move and this job marked the beginning of the road that led to the Prime Ministership; just as it signaled the disintegration of her marriage. "Although Morris and I remained married to each other and loving each other until the day he died in my house in 1951 (when, symbolically enough, I was away), I was not able to make a success of our marriage," she wrote in her memoirs.

Golda Meir has rarely displayed personal pride in the course of her long public career. And that is why I remember particularly a boastful remark she made at a State Dinner in her honor at the White House in 1973. After dessert was served, my father had given the traditional short welcoming speech and had toasted Mrs. Meir. In her responding toast, Golda told the assembled guests, "I can honestly say at least one thing, I never ran away from a difficult situation." Because she refuses to discuss her marriage and has written about it only sketchily, we will never know how much she agonized when she reached the point when compromise was impossible and she had to choose "duty" over husband and children.

There can be no doubt but that Golda Meir loved her family. But she had to be part of the world. In Clara Stern's words, Golda simply "always had to have a cause." Yet it must have been hard for her as she traveled for the labor organization to endure Sheyna's accusations that she was trying to be "a public person, not a homebody." And equally hard for Golda to learn to live with the rejoicing of her children when she was stricken with migraine headaches and unable to go to work.

Lou Kaddar, the effervescent French woman whose admiration for Mrs. Meir has led her to sacrifice much of her own life over the past quarter of a century in order to act as Golda's assistant, says quite frankly, "Golda tried to be a devoted mother, but she was not." Today, Golda's daughter will rarely leave her family for a night unless there is an emergency. When her mother cannot visit the kibbutz where Sarah lives, two and a half hours from Tel Aviv, Sarah will make the trip to Tel Aviv, but she usually insists on returning on the same day.

There were too many times in those years when the life or death of the country struggling to be Israel seemed to depend upon Golda's being away from home for days, weeks, even months at a time. Golda always went, but reluctantly. It was not that she minded the staggering demands of a job. When, as Minister of Labor, she had to find ways to feed and clothe 680,000 Jews who had come to Palestine from seventy countries at the end of World War II, she accepted the challenge without hesitation. What caused her anguish was being away from home, losing contact with family and friends. Their lives went on while she was away and she had to fit herself back into their patterns each time she returned. And there was something more, something deep within her that disturbed her each time she had to leave the country. She could not bear to be separated from the soil of Israel. Mrs. Meir has said that heroic "is not a word that I use easily or often," but she used it to describe the women from the developing nations of Africa who were willing to travel to foreign lands to learn the skills their own countries needed.

Since Golda's family found her involvement in government difficult to accept, it is remarkable that she had the strength to continue her career, a word that Mrs. Meir assiduously avoids. She is not a feminist. She deplores the invention of that "unfortunate term, 'women's lib.'" As a young woman who chose the kibbutz life in 1921, she wanted only an equal share of the burden. When I asked if she still rejects the idea of describing her working life as a career, her brief replies indicated that she thought the whole subject irrelevant. In clipped sentences, she said, "Work I did. But I did not choose a career like a medical career. I did not choose a profession."

"The government service? Politics?" I asked. "It all just happened?"

She nodded.

She sees her life as that of a woman doing a job, just as everyone should do something with her or his life. She is uncomfortable with the very notion of being a seeker of power. Women's issues are not of primary interest, or even very important to Mrs. Meir.

I remember when she was at the White House in 1973. Coffee was served in the Blue Room after the State Dinner and the room was jammed with the powerful and the famous trying to edge closer to Mrs. Meir, trying to catch the eye of the Israeli Ambassador or of my parents or of an aide, of anyone who would introduce them to her. Those who had been at White House dinners before knew that time was limited. The coffee ritual lasted only ten minutes. But Mrs. Meir spent most of those minutes talking to some young female military aides. The aides were excited—and rather embarrassed since their main duty was to locate those guests whom the State Department or the Israeli Embassy felt Mrs. Meir should meet and bring them up to her. But Golda wanted to talk to them. She was interested to learn that for the first time military women had been given duty at the White House, not because this was a breakthrough for women, but because it was a parallel to Israel, where both men and women serve in the armed forces.

She was Prime Minister in a nation in which no woman can testify in a religious court, which means that divorce is impossible without the consent of the husband. A country where the Orthodox males thank God daily that they were not born women. A country where abortion is illegal. In her five years as leader of Israel, she never gave priority to women's issues. She handled most questions about her sex lightly, as when she was asked how it felt to be appointed the first woman Foreign Minister. She replied, "I don't know. I was never a man Minister."

Leaders of other nations came to regard Golda as simply Prime Minister, not as a woman. And that is what she wanted. My father told me, "She never wanted to be treated like a woman, but like a leader." Secretary of State William Rogers once commented to French President Georges Pompidou on how curious it was that the two trouble spots in the world at the moment, India and Israel, were both governed by women. Pompidou arched his eyebrows and said, "Are you sure?" It was meant as a witticism, but there was a serious undertone—a respect for women who were totally in control in what traditionally were men's jobs.

When Golda speaks of the great women of Israel, she does not single out the women in Parliament or in the Labor Movement, the movers and the doers, but the mothers who hate war and yet willingly watch their children go to Israel's defense. To Golda, these are the truly great women.

Golda Meir's friends and associates in government see her as a very feminine woman, despite her achievements, despite her strength and outspoken honesty. The picture they painted for me was of a tender, womanly figure which went far beyond the familiar grandmotherly image. They see her as a sensitive person whom one wants to protect from criticism, from overworking, from pushing herself too far.

She has suffered from severe migraine headaches for years, so severe that she is often incapacitated for hours during an attack. The woman who thought nothing of dawn-to-dusk work on a desert kibbutz or of taking on a job that required constant travel, entertaining and decision-making is defenseless when migraine strikes. It is then that the kind-hearted woman who worries over her friends is in turn cared for by them. The room is darkened, the phone turned off, a sedative given. There is always someone to sit by her bed and hold her hand until she falls asleep. Someone to be there when she wakes up.

Golda's indomitable sense of duty was never described to me as an obsession, but as an admirable, lovable quality. This gray-haired woman with the painful legs and the cruel migraines has proved time and again that she can out-read, out-talk, out-smoke and out-think many younger men and women. But those who know her have a chivalrous attitude toward her, a desire to serve and protect. Her sometime driver, Danny, who is assigned to the Foreign Ministry and who helped me during my visit said, "Golda! I would give my life for that woman. That's all!"

People love Golda because she loves them. Danny told me about the day she gave him a ride to work. She was Foreign Minister then. On her way to the office, Golda passed Danny on the road. Golda, who as usual was in the front seat beside the driver, ordered the car stopped. Danny hopped in the back seat and they proceeded to the foreign office. The driver told Danny later that Golda had scolded him. "What's wrong with you?" she had asked. "Why didn't you stop? Didn't you see Danny?"

All her life Golda Meir has established intimate contacts with her working associates, her household help—even the soldiers assigned to guard her as Prime Minister. And in their turn, these young men became very attached to the woman for whom they were expected to give their lives if it proved necessary. They came to know the woman behind the Prime Minister.

On Saturdays, a holy day during which no government business is conducted, no official receptions or meetings held, she would often be home alone. The soldiers knew Golda hated solitude. And when they saw that she was alone, they would call her personal assistant, Lou Kaddar.

At eight-thirty the phone would ring in Lou's third-floor walk-up, not far from the Prime Minister's residence in Jerusalem.

Lou would know what it was before she picked up the receiver. "What time is it?" she would ask angrily, exhausted from a typical week of sixteen-hour days.

"Were you asleep, Lou?"

"Yes. Why are you calling me?" She knew perfectly well why they were calling.

"How would you like to spend the day with Golda?" All the soldiers called the Prime Minister "Golda."

"Go to hell," Lou would shout into the phone.

"How about nine-fifteen? We'll pick you up."

"No," Lou would say and hang up. But she would always be downstairs waiting at nine-fifteen. Lou spent many Saturdays in Golda's kitchen while Golda bustled about preparing good plain Jewish food for her. Despite the fact that French-born Lou does not care for anyone's good plain Jewish cooking, I got the impression that she enjoyed those Saturdays.

Golda has a gift for friendship. Although she is single-minded in her devotion to work and duty, she has had the ability to surround herself with people who are slightly irreverent and candid, like Lou Kaddar.

Before she became Prime Minister, Golda had never gone to a resort for a vacation, with the result that she found herself at a loss when her doctor ordered her to spend three days at a spa and get some rest. Lou Kaddar went with her, but every afternoon Lou would disappear for an hour or so. She told Golda she was going swimming. But Golda, who hated being alone possibly more than anything else and who could not imagine that anyone could want to go swimming alone, told Lou half-jokingly that she didn't believe she really spent all that time at the pool.

The last evening of her vacation Golda and Lou went for a walk, trailed as usual by security men. When they came to the pool, Golda said scornfully,

"There's your dear swimming pool. If you like to swim so much, why don't you go in now?"

Lou, fully clothed, jumped into the pool.

"Come out. Come out, Lou. You'll get a cold," Golda called frantically. She ordered her bodyguards to go for towels. Lou, her clothes ruined, decided to make the most of the opportunity to tease Golda and swam around until she was ready to come out.

When one realizes how much Golda Meir depends on others for companionship and stimulation, it is sad to read in her memoirs the many references to the joys and satisfactions of the kibbutz and her regret that she "did not find the strength" to return to the life of a close community. She has never forgotten her pioneering days as one of the settlers of Merhavia or the excitement of transforming the land by one's labor. When she told me about the journey that led from the United States to Merhavia so many years ago, she became animated. "I took none of my appliances or furnishings. I thought, 'I'll live in a tent. What do I need curtains for?' Oh, I was deliberate." Golda made sweeping gestures in cadence with her words. "No water. No electricity. Just rocks and swamps." She exulted in her description of the land she had chosen.

She left Merhavia in an effort to save her marriage, but she has always retained an idealized view of kibbutz life and sees it as "the solution for how men should live most fruitfully." During World War II, for example, she suggested that Palestine should become a kibbutz-like society with a network of cooperative kitchens so that at least the children would get enough to eat, but the idea was turned down. When she served as Israel's first Ambassador to the Kremlin, she ran the embassy like a kibbutz. She even cooked communal meals in her hotel room on weekends and washed the dishes in the bathroom, in the days before the Russians allotted them permanent quarters.

The kibbutz way of life appeals to many women because they can work and raise their children at the same time. Mrs. Meir is convinced that kibbutz parents spend more time with their children than many parents who live more traditional lives. Certainly there are no neglected children in the kibbutzim.

Clara told me of visiting her niece, Golda's daughter, at Revivim, the kibbutz where she has lived since 1946. At the time, there were ten babies in the nursery. Instead of going to her own baby, Sarah picked up another infant first and played with it for a few minutes. During the hour that they were in the nursery, five other mothers came in. Each picked up the same infant and cuddled it rather than going to their own babies first.

"What's so special about that baby?" Clara asked finally.

"Her mother died a few weeks ago," Sarah told her. The other women had become substitute mothers.

I made the journey to Revivim to meet Sarah and her husband and their two children and to see the community where Golda now has a small retirement apartment and where she can be, at least for a few days now and then, part of a larger community.

For two and a half hours I drove through the miles and miles of sand that separate Revivim from Jerusalem. There were vegetable fields and fruit groves at intervals, desert miracles made possible by irrigation. Revivim, which is Hebrew for dewdrops, is in the very heart of the Negev and had once been considered barren and uncultivable. The kibbutz was founded by seven young men, one of them Sarah's future husband, in 1943. They lived in a cave for the first two years. Despite irrigation with salty water, they could get nothing but palm trees to grow in the beginning. When Sarah joined the kibbutz three years later, life was still harsh, as it was to be for years to come.

Lou Kaddar had told me the story of how in 1956 several wealthy Jews from abroad had come to visit Revivim with the idea of making a financial contribution. Asked if they cared for any refreshments, the visitors said that all they would like was ice water. When they were told that it was not available, the visitors were terribly insulted and left the kibbutz. No one had a chance to explain that it was assumed they would not want to drink salty water.

Even today life in the middle of the Negev is not easy. At least once a week a sandstorm whirls across the cultivated acres and around the apartments of the five hundred people who live and work in Revivim. Sarah's daughter Naomi, a tiny, slender girl with long black hair, who looked too young and frail for her job taking care of the eight-year-olds, described what it is like when a storm comes stealthily in the night. You are awakened not so much by the howling wind, but by the feeling of sand which seeps in under the doors and through the window cracks and steadily covers the objects—and the people—within. Although Naomi shrugged in a gesture of acceptance, of "what can one do," I knew that each time she experienced the suffocating sensation of sand on her face and in her nostrils, it was as frightening as the first time. Naomi has lived on the kibbutz all her life and now that she is married continues to live and work there. She is accustomed to hardship, but it was obvious that one never grows accustomed to sandstorms.

Sarah Meir Rehabi has succeeded in living quietly in Revivim, despite the frequent visits of her famous mother. I discovered just how quietly when I arrived at the kibbutz and tried to find her apartment. I had picked up two young hitchhikers, paratroopers who were going to Revivim on weekend passes to spend the Sabbath with their families. I asked them how to get to Sarah's apartment, but when I followed their directions, I was told that Sarah had moved several months before. It took two more tries before I found someone who could lead me to the row of new apartments on the very edge of the settlement where she lived.

Knowing what Sarah had endured as one of the

pioneers of Revivim, I was eager to meet her. Sarah is a "sabra," the term used to describe a child born in Israel. In Hebrew it means prickly pear. Golda once said that one sees only the prickly exterior of the sabra, but that inside, like the pear, "they are juicy and sweet." The word seemed to apply particularly to Sarah, a self-controlled, quiet woman who seems to have great inner strength. She is as reserved as the descriptions of her father indicate he was and physically she resembles her father more than Golda. Her features are small. And her hair is black and curly like Naomi's.

She offered me fruit and a loaf cake that she had made the day before and we talked of kibbutz life; of the fresh challenge each day of trying to grow different fruits and vegetables, flowers, trees. There was no mention of my visit with her mother the previous day. And there were no photographs of her mother in the book-lined living room. But directly across the hall on the second floor of the four-family apartment unit in which Sarah lived was a door painted white like the others. This opened into Mrs. Meir's apartment, its three rooms the same size as her daughter's.

As I left I had a better understanding of why Golda Meir has said that children and grandchildren are the greatest blessing in life. And I was aware of the legacy she was leaving to Israel in the lives of Sarah and Menachem and their children and their children's children. To leave such a rich legacy to the future was sufficient personal ambition for Mrs. Meir.

It had been said that she became Prime Minister because she was without ambition. The men who had worked with her in building Israel knew that the woman they saw on the surface was the same woman underneath, not likely to change their goals because of new power. And her age placed her beyond long-term political plans. Looking back on her service as Prime Minister, Mrs. Meir confirmed what her colleagues had known all along. "I had no particular relish for the job," she said. "I never planned to be Prime Minister."

But she became Prime Minister, a Prime Minister who retained her down-to-earth manner and outlook. It is fascinating to read excerpts from the minutes of a Central Committee cabinet meeting. In the formal parliamentary language, the noting of "none opposed, four abstentions," it is refreshing to find the Prime Minister referred to as Golda. "The Central Committee earnestly appeals to Golda to retract . . ." Mrs. Meir had complete respect from her colleagues. It was just that she had always been Golda and Golda she would remain.

Her lifestyle remained practically unchanged despite the grandeur of the Prime Minister's residence. Her kitchen was still the center of her social life, the place where she enjoyed talking to friends and where she worked late into the night over briefing papers and documents once her friends had left. And almost inevitably it became the meeting place for other members of the government. Clara Stern, who frequently came to Jerusalem to stay with her sister, told me about a cabinet meeting that had lasted from eight at night to three the next morning. A Libyan jet pilot was flying over Israeli territory, asking for asylum. The cabinet members were summoned quickly. They sat around the dining-room table, the door to the kitchen open, and during the night-long discussions they wandered freely back and forth between the kitchen and dining room. Clara remembers that the Minister of Finance arrived without having had dinner. He went straight to the kitchen, opened the refrigerator door and stared helplessly at the contents until Clara suggested a tuna fish sandwich.

Golda usually had no help at night. The maid prepared the noonday meal, washed up and was gone by four. Fortunately, that particular evening Clara and Golda's eldest grandson were there to make the tea and coffee and serve the sandwiches and cakes. But one wonders how Golda managed to maintain her thread of thought and purpose on other similar occasions when there was no one to help her and, as hostess, she had to make the innumerable pots of coffee and set out the food.

Despite the informality of her kitchen "headquarters," Golda was in no way unprofessional about her job. When Clara visited her, the two sisters would always breakfast together. Clara, eager to learn as much as possible about what Golda was doing and about Israeli politics, would pepper her sister with questions. "But Golda never told me anything," she said when I visited her in Bridgeport. Clara worked out her own way of getting information from Golda. She would study the English-language *Jerusalem Post* over their breakfast of eggs and Arab flat bread and coffee, while Golda whipped through her own copy of the *Post* and the Tel Aviv newspapers, written in Hebrew. Clara would read an item from the *Post* out loud and then quickly glance up at Golda. "She wouldn't say a word," Clara told me, "but I would study her face. And then I'd know if something was going on."

Golda has never forgotten who she is or where she came from. Her first visit to Washington in 1969 when she had been Prime Minister for only six months illustrates the enormous contrasts in the woman who could bargain so confidently for her country and at the same time be so excited and awed by the ceremony surrounding her new position. The main purpose of her visit was to ask for twenty-five Phantom jets and other military hardware to be paid for with low interest loans. Lou Kaddar told me that she had never seen Golda more nervous than just before they reached Washington. "We needed those Phantoms," Lou said, "and it was her job to get them."

Golda was driven to the White House in the long black Presidential limousine, impressive with the small Israeli and American flags flapping briskly on each side. The Chief of Protocol, Bus Mosbacher, sat beside her. As the car entered the White House grounds and Golda saw the men in Army, Navy, Marine and Air Force uniforms lining the driveway, saw the band on the lawn and the platform near the house loaded with photographers and television equipment, she took Mosbacher's hand and held it tight as she said nervously, "Don't let me make a mistake. Don't let me make a mistake." Yet in her talks with my father after the official arrival ceremony, Golda forcefully presented Israel's case, with no trace of nervousness. My father said later that Golda "used her emotions. They didn't use her." And although she said that she would have to go back to the Knesset, the Israeli Parliament, for approval, she left no doubt that she was the one making the decisions.

But at the social climax of the visit, the State Dinner that followed the formal talks, Golda once more became the excited, emotional woman. She had tears in her eyes and a tender smile on her face when the Marine band played first the Israeli and then the American anthems. In the receiving line, between my parents, she looked startlingly small. Golda had such a presence, one never thought of her as being physically small.

My mother had been able to arrange for Leonard Bernstein and Isaac Stern to play for the Prime Minister and other guests after dinner. In the huge gold and white East Room, Golda sat between my parents in the center of the first row. Six-foot-tall portraits of George and Martha Washington, the President and First Lady whom Golda had learned about as a Russian emigrant schoolgirl in Milwaukee, hung on the walls. Photographers and reporters stood shoulder-to-shoulder at the back of the room and in both doorways. Their eyes and those of most of the one hundred dinner guests were trained on Israel's first woman Prime Minister. But Golda was oblivious of the attention, completely absorbed in the music. At the end, she impulsively hugged both Isaac Stern and

Leonard Bernstein, thanking them for having given so much beauty and pleasure.

She did not stay for the dancing, but went back to Blair House, the guesthouse for foreign visitors. Once in bed, she ordered coffee and then relived every detail of the evening with Lou Kaddar, who perched at the foot of the bed. Golda Meir rarely has had the opportunity or the inclination to pay attention to the small details of social events because her whole being is focused completely on the mission that prompted the parties and dinners. And so now, Lou, as she had so often in the past after other parties described the flowers, the antiques, the portraits, told Golda who was there and what they had worn. And, excited as a girl after a dance, Golda would ask, "Did he really say that, Lou?" "Oh, Lou, what did she wear?" on and on into the night.

Golda Meir is not a complicated person. She is forthright, strong and dedicated. Her outlook is dominated by one consideration—what is best for Israel. She asknowledges readily that the Jews have had a tragic history. Yet she has been able to work to make life better for her people. To her way of thinking, the only way to deal with adversity is as clear as the contrast between black and white. You give in—or you fight. And Golda is in her element when she is faced with a situation in which she can fight. But the personal tragedies of life—the illness which strikes down a friend, the senseless suffering of another person, the sudden death of a colleague—are much more difficult to deal with than the problems of feeding or clothing a million people or coolly arguing across the negotiating table with an intransigent enemy.

Because she is an uncompromising idealist, she finds it difficult to accept imperfection and impossible to forgive. She has said she will never forgive the Germans, nor the Arabs for certain atrocities, not even Ben-Gurion for the positions he took in some of their political disputes. She is not forgiving of herself either.

Whenever she refers to her failed marriage, she places the blame on herself. When one realizes that her life-long philosophy has been that nothing is impossible, one understands how soul-shattering this personal failure above all others must be to her still.

She is an idealist who has never sought power or fame. Instead she has sought purpose and duty. She is an idealist who believes the spiritual strength of the Jews is "indestructible and eternal." An idealist who believes man is master of his fate. More than half a century ago, she wrote a friend in New York, "I was happy I saw a naked rock. You see, some day when there is a forest along this road, I will know and everyone will know that those trees will be there because we planted them."

Even now as age and disappointment weigh heavily on her, Golda continues to be an idealist. And an optimist. She says that only the old in Israel are optimists, because only the old can really know how far the country has come since the first kibbutz settlements.

"How can one make the younger generation more optimistic?" I asked. "And how in this midst of increasing materialism can Israel keep alive the Zionist spirit of a just society?"

"There is no recipe," she answered simply. "But we are a young country. We can still see evidence of the pioneer spirit. That is important."

As we talked, I sensed that she had faith, not so much in the young, but in Israel, the land and what it stood for. Perhaps without her realizing it, Golda Meir is vitally important to any spark of optimism among the young. It was her idealism and spirit which first drew me to her and made me eager to know more about her beliefs and her life. I will never forget the remarks she made at the White House in 1969. After the talk with my father she declared that she would return home to Israel and tell her cabinet, her people, her children—"Don't become cynical. Don't give up hope. Don't believe that everything is judged only by expediency. There is idealism in this world. There is human brotherhood."

There was a great deal of suppressed emotion as we ended our visit together. It was the day after the third anniversary of Israel's third war since statehood, the war which compelled her to say, "I will never again be the same person I was before the Yom-Kippur War." Twenty-five hundred Israelis were killed in that war. Critics claim that she could have prevented the war if she had called for a general alert in the country. As I sat facing her that morning in her small office, I could only try to imagine the pain and rejection she must feel. The accusations and repercussions were the major cause of her resignation seven months later. It seemed cruel, after her long life of struggle and achievement, for Golda to have to sit out her retirement years in the shadow of the Yom-Kippur War.

When I asked if she could tell me anything about the war, she said, "We did not have the proper intelligence," and then her voice trailed off and she sat silent. It was obvious that she still was unable to reveal more than what she had written in her autobiography: "There is still a great deal which cannot be told." But it was not just her inability to divulge information that was still classified. Golda did not want to discuss this time in her life that had been so painful and often beyond her control; the months that had extinguished the fire I had once seen in her eyes.

It was equally difficult for me to talk about the man who had brought us together, who was the reason Golda Meir had agreed to see me. When she asked, "How is your father? Is he writing every day? What is he doing now?" I started to describe the progress of his autobiography. But other thoughts ran through my mind as I talked. The isolation and loneliness of San Clemente. How my father seemingly was condemned to a life of inaction. I thought of all Golda Meir and my father had done for what they hoped would be a lasting peace. Their efforts were a thing of the past now. They would never again work together.

Suddenly, though my words were still about his writing, my voice broke and there were tears in my eyes. I looked down at my notepad. But I made no pretense of turning the pages, of searching for some last question. I was silent. Golda was silent, too.

Later, after we had touched lightly on other topics and I had regained a steady voice, I asked her, "Why is it that some people seem to have fewer obstacles and tragedies in their lives than others?" She did not answer. Perhaps her answer came a few minutes later when she impulsively put her arms around me to kiss me good-bye. Her answer to the vicissitudes of life is compassion, not words.

Golda Meir had begun our visit with concerned questions about my mother's health. And her very last words were of my mother. Golda told me to take warm greetings back home. And then she shook her head as if the words were not enough. She wanted to say more. "Your mother is a wonderful person. Through all that period I kept asking, 'How did she endure it all? How did she endure it all?'"

I am surprised that Golda asked the question. For she knows the answer. "Nothing in life just happens," she said once. "You have to have the stamina to meet obstacles and overcome them. To struggle." And that is how Golda Meir has lived her life, working for Israel, struggling to make a dream come true.

Ruth
Bell
Graham

"Yea, I have loved thee with
an everlasting love: therefore with
lovingkindness have I drawn
thee."—Jeremiah 31:3

Her Bible is so worn and soft that Ruth Bell Graham can roll it like a magazine. She turns each page gently so it will not tear. And each page is familiar. She has read and reread it in moments of happiness, moments of pain, when she was seeking answers, and when she was merely expectant. The hundreds of underlined verses and the margins filled with tightly written notations, some in pencil, some in blue or black ink, attest to the extraordinary way in which Ruth Graham communicates with God.

The first time I saw Ruth's Bible was just before Christmas in 1973. The Grahams had spent Saturday night at the White House as guests of my parents, and on Sunday Billy Graham preached at the interdenominational church service in the East Room. After dinner on Saturday, I had asked Ruth if we could visit together before church the next morning.

I had always been fascinated by Ruth Graham. Her husband is a famous evangelist who has delivered the message of God to millions of people, yet Ruth seems more comfortable when sharing her faith in God quietly, face to face with another seeker. She is spiritual, but at the same time spirited and very much a part of this world. How many other grandmothers take up hang-gliding in their fifties? Ruth did. And the first time she jumped off Maggie Valley Mountain she had barely recovered from injuries caused by falling out of a tree when she was putting up a swing for her grandchildren, injuries so severe that it was a week before she regained consciousness. And how many grandmothers borrow their son's black leather jacket and go vrooming along mountain roads on a Harley-Davidson? A daring driver, Ruth (and her motorcycle) ended up in a ditch once, in a lake another time.

The Grahams had been friends of my parents for over twenty years and though I had talked to Ruth many times before, we had never discussed her faith. This time was different. I was very much aware of the quiet assurance she found in God. I envied it. I wanted to know how Ruth, a woman with spunk and a strong will, could yield her life so completely to God. What gave her the faith to pray about the small things in her life and the large? To pray and to believe that God listens? That God answers?

The third floor of the White House was very quiet that Sunday morning. The domestic staff was busy downstairs preparing the coffee and pastries that would be served after Dr. Graham's sermon. Ruth and I talked in the little sitting room next to their bedroom. It was dark and gloomy despite the bright December sunshine outside. The balustrade that circles the White House roof blocked the sun, and because of its columns the rays that did penetrate the room fell like bars across the furniture and rug. But Ruth seemed radiant, despite the dark room and the fact that she and Billy had stayed up late the night before talking with my mother and father. She laughed as she unbuckled the strap that held her Bible together and excused the worn appearance of the book. The thin black strap looked like a belt and Ruth said that was exactly what it was, a woman's belt that she had cut down for this very purpose. I was startled by her hands as she fingered the pages of her Bible. They were extremely lined and rough. The only touch of elegance was the wide gold wedding band. But Ruth's hands were capable, surely strong enough to guide a motorcycle or hang, high over the valley, on to her gliding kite.

My questions came rapidly, all at once:

"How do you study the Bible?"

"How do you learn from it?"

"Why all the seeming inconsistencies? Why so many instances of cruelty?"

"Why do you believe in it so deeply?"

Ruth listened quietly until I paused. Then with a smile she said, "I'll try the scatter-gun approach." She held the book in her lap and slowly turned the pages until she came to passages which had meaning for her. I was surprised by her casual, random search, this thumbing through pages, but Ruth explained, "God doesn't deal with people in a formulated way. We shouldn't either." And this was a message she reinforced several times. As I listened, I realized that she offered no easy answers. There were no three steps to comfort or a formula for faith in Ruth Graham's approach. There was nothing pat about her response to my questions.

"It's surprising that there aren't more inconsistencies in the Bible," Ruth said as she leafed through the pages. "So many different people wrote it. And from so many different points of view. It's the differences that make it valid. You know the old story about the four blind men and the elephant. One man held the tail and told his companions that it was a rope. Another ran his hands over the body of the elephant and insisted that it was a wall. The third put his arms around the elephant's leg and said it was a tree trunk. The fourth touched the elephant's trunk and believed it was a snake.

"But in the Bible, none of these differences between the people who wrote it affect the great doctrines."

She turned to the back of her Bible and stopped at Chapter Eight of Romans. She read out loud to me, "Who shall separate us from the love of Christ? shall tribulation, or distress, or persecution, or famine, or nakedness, or peril, or sword?" She paused for a moment and then said quietly, "Only sin, sin which touches every man and woman, separates us from God's love." Then she turned to an earlier verse in Romans and read, "For all have sinned, and come short of the glory of God."

As she spoke those words, Ruth was already eagerly turning back to Isaiah. She read the fifth verse of the Fifty-third Chapter, substituting her own name, "But he was wounded for Ruth's transgressions, he was bruised for Ruth's iniquities: the chastisement of our peace was upon him; and with his stripes, Ruth is healed." She read the words with emotion, her voice almost caressing each syllable, in a Southern accent so marked that it was almost unbelievable that Ruth, the daughter of missionary parents, spoke Chinese before she learned English. She wanted me to know and be assured of the gift of God's love.

"But let's look at the Psalms," Ruth said. "I always draw great help and comfort from them." As she turned page after page, it seemed as if every other verse were underlined. It was apparent that each of them had spoken to her in a special way. When she reached the Thirty-seventh Psalm, Ruth laughed softly. "I've set up camp in Psalm Thirty-seven." She ran her finger down the page and stopped at the fourth verse. "This is the one I think I love more than all others," and she read, "Delight thyself also in the Lord; and he shall give thee the desires of thine heart."

"My favorite translation is from the Septuagint Bible," she said. "It goes—'Indulge thyself also in the Lord.' I love that thought of indulging myself in the Lord. Really, the main thing in studying the Bible," she said, "is to get into it and enjoy it."

At ten-thirty, when Ruth and I had to stop to get ready for the service, I left her with two strong impressions after our hour and a half together. She was not at all a brittle, upbeat Christian who denied all doubts or questions. And she undeniably enjoyed great inner peace. She had not answered all my questions, but somehow that seemed less important now. I was eager to know more about the Bible, and about Ruth herself.

The next time I saw Ruth Graham's shabby, cherished Bible was at the San Diego Crusade in August, 1976. Ruth shared it with me during the scripture reading that preceded Dr. Graham's sermon. She had hesitated before moving it a few inches closer to me so that I, too, could follow the lesson, and so I tried to focus my eyes on the verses and not let them wander to her marginal notations. I understood that these were as personal as a diary, for her eyes alone. I was not surprised by her reluctance to reveal her spiritual journey. A few months earlier, she had tried to dissuade me from writing about her, warning me in a letter that, "I feel a bit like someone doing a strip-tease when there's really not that much to show."

We were seated in the third row of a section of the stadium slightly to the right of the speaker's platform, lost in the anonymity of the crowd. The people around us were unaware that Ruth Graham was in their midst. Five minutes before, Ruth and Billy had quietly walked across the grassy field. Billy Graham never makes a formal entrance and I did not know that he and Ruth were on the stadium grounds until she slipped into the seat next to me.

She was very detached from the huge apparatus that made the telecast of the crusade possible—the scores of team members milling about, the formidable rows of local ministers sitting on the platform, the choir of several hundred, the cameras and sophisticated lighting and sound equipment. While everyone else was still preparing for the event, Ruth was already well into it. She did not look around the audience for her friends and staff members. She gazed at her husband on the platform. And she was silent. I knew she and Billy had been praying for months for the success of the crusade. I was sure that she was praying then as well.

Despite Ruth's attempts to separate herself from the nonspiritual aspects of the crusade while in the city where it was held, her husband's lifestyle and, therefore her own, is similar to that of many important and powerful individuals whose time is precious, whose staff members are numerous and whose lives are in need of special protection. The atmosphere surrounding the Grahams that evening had reminded me strongly of a Presidential campaign. When I arrived at their motel, there was the familiar motorcade, the cars all lined up in readiness for the drive to the stadium. There was the police motorcycle escort, gloved and goggled, ready for the signal to start. A member of the Graham team was in constant walkie-talkie communication with the evangelist's top-floor suite. Bunny Graham Dienert, my good friend, took me to her parents' rooms. Standing watch outside was T. W. Wilson, who has been a friend of Billy's ever since they were boys. I had a feeling I had been there before. Even their suite looked like a thousand other motel rooms I had walked into during my father's campaigns.

One difference, however, was Ruth's Bible, held together with the same thin belt, ready to take to the meeting that evening. Their eldest grandchild, Stephen, was with them. He is tall and dark with deepset eyes like his grandfather's. It was hard to realize that Ruth and Billy, who look as if they are in their early forties instead of their fifties, had a twelve-year-old grandson.

We made small talk for a few minutes. Bunny teased her mother by saying that she was surprised Ruth was on time for the crusade. Bunny had telephoned her early that morning to see if Ruth wanted to have breakfast with her, only to discover that her mother had already left for Mexico with a man she had never met, a former convict who had been in and out of prisons since he was eight years old. Ruth had started corresponding with him shortly after his release from San Quentin two years before. He had spent eleven years there as an incorrigible, leading an animal-like existence. Three times a day his food was deposited in his cell by a shovel device with a handle long enough to extend through the two security doors. Nevertheless, it was at San Quentin that he committed his life to God and to rehabilitation work among ex-convicts. That morning in Mexico he had shown Ruth some of the halfway houses he had established for prisoners.

We said very little after Ruth had described her trip. I felt the familiar air of tension, the waiting to get on with something important. I knew, too, that Billy Graham had spent most of the day alone, eating almost nothing, preparing for the evening. Finally, it was time to leave. It was a relief to have the waiting over.

There was a police checkpoint at the entrance to the stadium and we drove directly to an underground area. Several people were there waiting anxiously for Ruth. Some were strangers. Others, including a friend of Bunny's, an alcoholic who was then in her fourth marriage, had met with Ruth when she first arrived in San Diego. Ruth had counseled them and prayed for them all week. There was another small, insistent group of people clustered around Billy Graham's trailer. He disappeared inside to meet with those who needed to talk with him, to have "only one minute" of prayer, just like those people who insist on a minute of the political candidate's time even when he must gather his thoughts for the speech ahead.

But when Billy Graham emerged from his trailer and walked across the stadium field with his wife, the resemblance to a political campaign stopped. No one noticed him. There were no cheers. No laudatory introductions of the speaker. Dr. Graham was one of some forty ministers on the platform. As the time neared for the service to begin, people became subdued and contemplative. And, like Ruth, they became expectant.

When I had watched crusades on television, Billy Graham loomed large. He was inescapable on the television screen. His eyes very blue and penetrating, his lips moving very fast. But in San Diego he was a small figure dwarfed by the vast stadium. He was mostly a voice.

When he finished speaking, he asked people to come forward to acknowledge their belief in Christ as their personal Savior. Stillness fell over the stadium. The only sound was the soft organ music.

Then a handful of people started to walk across the field. I looked up and saw movement at the top of the bleachers. Tiny figures, far away, began the long journey down narrow aisles. There were hundreds of people moving forward now—the man in a three-piece suit holding his small son by the hand; an elderly couple, the woman with a cane, supporting each other as they walked slowly toward the platform; there were teenagers holding hands; people walking alone.

These people were not responding to a man. They certainly were not mesmerized by the small figure of Billy Graham standing at the edge of the platform. There was no fever pitch of emotion in the crowd. Something far greater was at work. I understood Ruth's words now. "It isn't a culture or a personality responding to a program or a man," she had told me before the crusade, "but the soul responding to the God who created it."

Everywhere Ruth goes she meets men and women whose lives have changed because of a crusade. When an earthquake devastated Guatemala in 1976, Ruth and Billy Graham flew there, carrying supplies for the survivors. An hour after their plane had taken off for the trip home, it received a radio communication from a tiny Cessna hundreds of feet below them. The pilot had attended a crusade ten years before and as a result had become a missionary. He was on his way to Guatemala, bringing food and medicine and clothing, to help pull bodies out of the rubble, and to try to nourish the souls and bodies of those who had survived.

The question Ruth Graham is asked most frequently is, "Do they last?" How many of those who come forward night after night, year after year at crusades really begin a study of the Bible and try to follow the teachings of Christ? It is impossible to cite statistics, but one thing is certain—while Billy Graham can deliver the "invitation," he must depend on others to encourage those who have been evangelized. That is why it takes a full year to prepare for a crusade. Counselors have to be trained to talk to people at the crusade. Leaders have to be found to conduct Bible study groups afterward. Local churches must be encouraged to offer various follow-up programs. Ruth corresponds with those who seek her spiritual help, and she prays for the others with all the urgency implied in Chapter Four of Ecclesiastes, verse ten— ". . . if they fall, the one will lift up his fellow: but woe to him that is alone when he falleth; for he hath not another to help him up." That verse is particularly meaningful to Ruth because she realizes the new converts have little chance of maintaining their dedication without continuing personal guidance and encouragement to study the Bible.

Ruth does not pray solely for the people who have found faith through a crusade. Her prayers go out in many directions. She told me that she has prayed for Eldridge Cleaver ever since she read his autobiography, *Soul on Ice*, in which he described how he had raped every white woman he could, because he was so filled with hate and bitterness over the injustice of his life as a black man. Today, Cleaver is a committed Christian. He has been appearing recently at Word of

Life rallies, testifying to his deep and growing faith, but Ruth's hope is that he will allow himself a quiet period for spiritual growth, a chance "to get into the scriptures and memorize them." She thinks it is important that he resist pressure from those who want to push him into the limelight, speaking and writing about his faith.

Her concern is based upon experience. "Too often," Ruth says, "we Christians, and that includes those at the crusades, put up a brand-new Christian to share his faith. Shortly afterward, he becomes discouraged or has doubts. It's like a child learning to walk. They fall a lot and you help them up again and little by little they become confident." She is convinced that a quiet growing period is necessary. "Even St. Paul disappeared for several years," she points out, "while he grounded himself in his new faith."

As the wife of an evangelist, Ruth Graham is expected to be ready and willing to offer spiritual advice to those who write to her and to those who seek her out in person. But there are times when Ruth herself is spiritually bereft: she still believes in God, but finds that she can no longer pray easily and spontaneously. These episodes of what she calls "spiritual dryness" always follow very busy periods when she does not have time to study the Bible on a regular basis. "It is just as if Bill and I get so busy and go for several days and don't sit down and have a good talk," she explained. At that moment I realized how much Ruth has sacrificed to the demands of her husband's ministry. There were many years when she could not travel with her husband because of the children, times when weeks and sometimes months would go by without her having the opportunity for "a good talk" with Billy.

I visited the Grahams at their mountaintop home in Montreat in North Carolina a month after the San Diego Crusade. Ruth picked me up at the airport in Asheville after my "puddle-jump" flight from New

York, which had made two stops before touching down in Asheville. Montreat is tucked away in the Black Mountains, not an easily accessible crossroads despite the fact that it is the home of one of the most sought-after men in the world.

As we approached the house, Ruth used the radio intercom to let her husband know we were almost there. As soon as she had finished transmitting, Billy came on. "I know," he said. "We've been hearing a very interesting conversation for the last five minutes." The microphone had rolled into a crack between the car seats in such a way that the intercom button was depressed. The result was that no one could reach us and inform us that our chatter was being overheard. It must have been an amusing five minutes. Ruth and I had talked about the weather, the merits of several crusade staff members, and the arthritic problems of a mutual friend which somehow had led to a discussion of hot flashes. When we learned that we had had an audience (the radio is also hooked up to aide T. W. Wilson's house) we laughed so hard that tears rolled out of the corners of my eyes. Ruth was doubled over the wheel and for a few seconds, despite the dizzying curves of the mountain road, she pumped the accelerator wildly because she could not stop laughing. We were still laughing when Ruth drove through the electronically controlled gate for the final climb up the steep, winding road to the house.

The Grahams' house is made of hand-hewn logs from old abandoned cabins. The world of commercialism and cynicism seemed remote in this corner of the Black Mountains. The kitchen is the heart of the house, a large room, its walls and ceilings, like those of all the other rooms, of exposed timber. A fire blazed on the open hearth. A colorful rag rug covered the brick floor and pewter jugs dented with years of use were hung on wooden pegs. It would be hard not to feel at home in the Grahams' kitchen. But the whole house was equally simple and welcoming. A hall window was filled with glass bottles. When I admired an especially pretty dark blue bottle, Ruth told me it was a Milk of Magnesia bottle minus its label.

The room I liked almost as much as the kitchen was my own, the spare bedroom. It invited a guest to relax, to sleep late—to be at peace. Everything was simple, but designed for a guest's comfort. Ruth kept a coffeemaker on the closet shelf so that guests could have that first cup of coffee in the morning without having to dress and go to the kitchen. There was another braided rag rug on the wide-plank floor. And another fireplace with the logs laid ready for a match. On the chest of drawers beside the bed was a row of books including a history of China, several works by C. S. Lewis, and a *Daily Light,* which contains scripture verses for each day of the year. Surprisingly there was no Bible.

My bed was huge—and high. I had to use a two-step wooden stair to climb in. I hoped that I would not be restless during the night. It would be a hard landing if I were to roll out of bed. Underneath was a trundle bed for the grandchildren. A koala bear and a green stuffed walrus were tucked away in the closet for their visits.

Ruth Graham's parents had settled in Montreat when they returned from China at the beginning of World War II. And because Billy traveled so much, Ruth chose to raise her children in this beautiful and peaceful community. It is the place, Billy says, where he most often finds renewal because he has more time when he is home to study the Bible and to think.

Everything is geared to Billy when he is in Montreat. Ruth refuses to have a firm schedule when Billy is there. "Being married to Bill, I have to hang loose and play it by ear," she told me. And then she laughed, "I tell my friends I have become a very loose woman indeed!" The daily routine was carefully designed around her husband during my visit. On Saturday, we ate our large meal of the day at noon. Ruth and the caretaker's wife, who helps with the housework, did the cooking. But the rest of Saturday and all day Sunday we were completely alone enjoying the peace and privacy that Billy looks forward to so much on the weekends when he is home.

Their house in Montreat offers more than privacy to the Grahams. It offers physical security. They had to move out of the little town up to their mountaintop twenty years ago when it became impossible to cope with the tourists who would walk into the yard, take photographs of the children, even look in the windows. People often arrived at the front door demanding to see Billy and then were extremely unhappy, sometimes quite unpleasant, if, as was often the case, he was not at home. Their present property, which they bought for five dollars an acre, is surrounded by an eleven-foot-high fence, erected at the suggestion of the F.B.I. after the assassination of Martin Luther King, Jr., a time when there was an alarming increase in the number of threats on Billy Graham's life.

Yro, their German-trained German shepherd, is probably even better security than the fence. He is a very large, very powerful animal. I was quite wary of him at first because I could not communicate with him. Yro responds only to German commands. Around Ruth and Billy, however, he was an affectionate and happy house dog. Much too well-trained to beg and whine at the door, he would look at us with mournful eyes whenever he was not allowed to come into the house. Saturday night, when we were eating supper in the kitchen—Ruth's good homemade soup, cheese and crackers—Yro put his nose on the table to survey our meal better. Billy gruffly commanded him to *platz,* lie down, and Yro obeyed meekly.

The fence, the dog and the radio communications setup between car and home are all security precautions urged on the Grahams by concerned friends and staff. The Grahams themselves have a casual attitude toward it all. Ruth, in fact, jokes that her guardian angel is "highly insulted," especially by the fence. She and Billy tend to turn the security measures into toys, just as Yro has become a rather lazy, sleep-by-the-fire pet.

The morning after I arrived, Ruth and I went for a hike. With Yro and a marshmallow fork to protect us against copperheads and rattlesnakes, we climbed up the mountain behind their house. I had to concentrate so hard on the thorny blackberry bushes and the thick "touch-me-not" vines that became entangled around my feet and legs that I did not worry much about snakes. And anyway, Ruth had assured me that we would get a little warning—according to her mountain neighbor, Dad Roberts, snakes smell like cucumbers.

Ruth set a fast pace up an incline that seemed almost perpendicular to me. "Let me know when you want to stop to rest," she said. I was sure she would call a halt before I did, but finally, rather sheepishly, I suggested we sit for a while on a log in an opening that was just "too picturesque" to pass by. The aspens and maples still had their leaves and the thick branches created a private world in which we talked. Here on the mountain, we seemed to be able to see each other more clearly than before and to talk more freely.

I asked Ruth about those times when she had told me she felt separated from God, when the words "my soul cleaveth into the dust" seemed to be vividly true.

"I think of the time Bill and I were in Lausanne for a conference on World Evangelism," she said. "I was constantly meeting new people. Most of them had asked to see me. They wanted spiritual advice. After a few days, I was exhausted. It became a real ordeal. My ability to pray almost disappeared while I was in Switzerland."

She had not had time for quiet daily study of the Bible for several weeks before the trip. And when she did turn to the Bible again, she said, "I hardly knew where to begin. I felt as dry as a bone. Finally I started to read the Psalms."

It was the One Hundred and Nineteenth Psalm that caught her attention. In her hotel room, she read and reread it from every perspective. She pondered on what the psalmist himself felt—his fears, his temptations, his despairs, his hopes. "My soul melteth for heaviness: strengthen thou me according unto thy word. . . . Teach me, O Lord, the way of thy statutes . . . Give me understanding, and I shall keep thy law . . . Incline my heart unto thy testimonies . . . Behold, I have longed after thy precepts: quicken me in thy righteousness."

And she thought long about what God was saying through the psalm, of His promise of shelter and nourishment. "Thy word is a lamp unto my feet, and a light unto my path." "How sweet are thy words unto my taste! yea, sweeter than honey to my mouth." And finally she thought about what God's word requires of man. "My lips shall utter praise . . . My tongue shall speak of thy word: for all thy commandments are righteousness . . . thy law is my delight." Slowly renewal came and Ruth felt grateful that she could open her Bible, despite the weeks of perfunctory reading, and find encouragement.

Experiences like this have made Ruth eager for others to find God and stay near Him by studying his word. She has long been aware of the urgency of those people seeking answers who have thronged to the crusades, but it is only recently that politicians and the press have discovered that the Evangelical Christians, estimated to number seventy-eight million Americans, are big news—and a potentially powerful political force when united in belief.

That evening both Ruth and Billy spoke of their concern that the present wave of newly "born again," people who have experienced a spiritual renewal, may be exploited by "road-show" ministers who promise miracles, or may be ridiculed by the media.

We were sitting in the kitchen and had pulled our easy chairs close to the fire blazing on the open hearth.

I felt very much at home in this isolated log house. It seemed unbelievable that Billy Graham would be leaving Montreat on Monday to pick up the role of a visible public figure, a role that he more and more reluctantly accepts. The uncomplicated desire that Billy and Ruth first shared to proclaim the message of God's love and forgiveness has become inextricably linked to a public image forged in part by Billy's daily newspaper column and his books—almost a book a year. The burden of this public role is made even more complex by the numerous films and publications of the Billy Graham Evangelistic Association. Administrative decisions for the Association are made by an independent board, but ultimately Billy Graham shoulders the responsibility for what is done in his name.

The public relations and publicity that are necessary to proclaim the Gospel to the world are a source of tension in their lives. Twenty years ago at one of the first televised crusades when there was a great deal of interest in Billy and his family, Ruth wrote her parents, "I will be so glad when the press gets all its stories written and the publicity dies down so that we can get on with the message." They both believe that it is the message that is crucially important, not the man who brings the message. He is simply the instrument.

Ruth married a man whose glorious gift she believed was his ability to preach the news of salvation. They both wanted the message to reach as many people as possible. But neither Ruth nor Billy ever dreamed that his ministry would be larger than any man's in the history of Christianity. More than one hundred million people have heard Billy Graham preach. The growth of his ministry seems almost like a miracle to Ruth. As the child of medical missionary parents, she heard her mother and father pray daily to God, asking Him to send them more people to "save," people from beyond the boundaries of the small town of Tsingkiangpu, where they had built a hospital. Today, just three nights of a televised crusade result in more than half a million letters from those who watch and listen and sometimes kneel to pray by their television sets.

I asked Ruth if she had ever dreamed when she met Billy at Wheaton College in Illinois that his career would bring such power and fame. She smiled and answered, "No, I wouldn't have had the nerve to marry him." It was a flip answer, one that I knew she had given before. But Ruth did not stop there. She hesitated, her face became thoughtful and then she said, "God has the wisdom not to let us see ahead."

The couple whose one-week honeymoon at Blowing Rock, North Carolina, had cost seventeen dollars could not have foreseen the pinpricks that come with celebrity, such as the news accounts that imply they lead a rich life with Billy wearing three-hundred-dollar suits. In truth, he is a perfect size 42 long and Ruth buys his clothes at Sears. His newest suit, with two pairs of pants, cost seventy-five dollars. "I tell myself that since Bill is trying to do the Lord's work, it's the Lord's problem to handle the criticism," Ruth said. But it was obvious that the rumors about personal extravagances and hidden bank accounts in Switzerland and South America really hurt. They try to deflate such stories by publishing Dr. Graham's salary every year. It is $39,000. And he accepts no honorariums for speaking.

Billy told me, "I would give almost anything not to be recognized. I would not be on television for anything except God's work." The strain of the quarter century of crusades held all over the world has taken its toll. Billy has never recovered from the New York crusade in 1957 when for sixteen weeks he spoke, sometimes twice a night to capacity crowds in Madison Square Garden. More than two and a quarter million people attended those meetings. Billy lost thirty-seven pounds. Even harder than the physical strain was the struggle to find the time and the quiet for meditation and studying the Bible so that his sermons would not become mechanical or unthinking. In recent years, although the crusades last only a week, Ruth says, "Bill is totally washed out after each one."

I had not known before that Ruth was concerned about her husband's health. He looks vigorous and strong, but they estimate that he will not have the physical stamina to continue the crusades for more than another six or seven years. He will then have to cut down and adopt a less grueling schedule. High blood pressure haunts him as it haunted his father, who died at age sixty-five. Billy takes medicine to help control the condition and tries to exercise regularly. He jogs a mile in the afternoon, rain or shine, whenever he can manage to find the time. At home in Montreat, he also swims in the small pool that Ruth had built for him a few years ago during one of his long absences. The pool, directly off the bedroom, is very small—four strokes long by two strokes wide—but when Billy returned home and discovered Ruth's surprise, he was provoked and unhappy. She handled the situation with her usual spirited teasing, telling him, "It's cheaper than a funeral."

Saturday afternoon when I saw him come back from his run, looking slim in his bright-red turtleneck and jeans, I never would have believed that he had to watch his health so carefully. He does not appear any older than he did ten years ago—and he is not at all enthusiastic about a grandmotherly image for Ruth. At his insistence, she colors her shoulder-length hair. Ruth is candid about her new look. She laughed as she showed me a snapshot taken outside their house the previous year. Billy is looking down at her hair and saying something. She is laughing.

"Bill is telling me for the tenth time that month that my hair would look a whole lot prettier in the sunshine if it were brown instead of gray." After a little more friendly persuasion, Ruth accepted her husband's suggestion. As I watched the two of them together—the zest of their relationship, the teasing, the quick understanding—I felt sad to think that they face the very real possibility of only a few more years of marriage.

I mentioned this—it is easy to talk to the Grahams about any subject, even their own mortality. Neither of them was troubled by the idea of death. Ruth told me frankly that she is glad that the number of evangelists is increasing every year. "If Bill dropped dead tomorrow, there would be many to take his place." The Grahams accept death. They believe God will call them "home" when He wants them and not a minute earlier.

When Billy does start cutting down, Ruth wants him to give up the crusades and concentrate on television. "You can reach people that way who would never set foot inside a crusade," she says urgently. She believes it is vitally important to reach the greatest number of people possible because "If God does not judge America, He will have to send a letter of apology to Sodom and Gomorrah." She is serious. She is firmly convinced that judgment of the United States has been delayed as long as it has only because Americans have sent so many missionaries around the world.

She is also convinced that more than anything else in life, we need a sense of forgiveness, whether it be for a sin against a friend or an overt crime, because no man is without sin. She smiled as she illustrated her point. "Years ago, Edward R. Murrow visited us to film a segment for his program *Person to Person*. I spent two days cleaning house and getting ready," Ruth said. "Then the television crew came and set up their lights. When they turned them on, it was awful. You have never seen more cobwebs and dust in your life." She ended her story saying, "We think we are pretty good because we have not yet stood in the light of God's glory."

She told another story, a moving one about meeting a young girl named Wendy during a month-long crusade in London. Wendy, a heavy drug user, came to the crusade night after night, but she was still not committed, still searching. Wendy and Ruth had many talks together. One evening before the service began, Ruth told the girl, "One day you will come to something difficult in your life. And then—you will either go back on drugs or go on with Christ."

A few days before the end of the crusade, Ruth was sitting in the stadium at Earls Court when someone passed her a note from Wendy. "I am on drugs," she read. "Come help me." When Ruth found Wendy by the stadium entrance, she was almost unconscious. A girl with her explained that Wendy's best friend had died from an overdose that afternoon. Ruth took a package of Kleenex from her handbag, the only paper she could find, and on its cardboard backing she quickly wrote,

"God loves me.

"Jesus died for me.

"No matter what I've done, if I confess to Him, He will forgive me."

She tucked the cardboard in Wendy's pocket and then one of the crusade staff members took the girl home. A year later, Ruth met Wendy again in London. Wendy asked Ruth about the note she had found in her pocket. She had no recollection whatsoever of having asked Ruth for help, but that message Ruth had left with her had been her lifeline to God, she said.

Ruth believes with all her heart in that simple message she gave Wendy. The act of confession and acceptance of God's love means that no man need suffer the cruel fate of hell. And hell is very real to Ruth. She describes it as "eternal separation from God."

Ruth was the main researcher for Billy's 1953 best seller, *Peace with God,* and she had combed the Bible for definitions of hell. They were frightening—"intense darkness," "rubbish and debris," "place of judgment and suffering." That is why Ruth says with great feeling, "I don't want Bill to be diverted from what God wants him to do. It's so easy to be diverted." And she spoke of there always being cornerstones to be laid, advertising clubs to be addressed and, most of all, politics and politicians.

"Don't advertising men and politicians need the news of salvation?" I asked.

"Bill's job is to reach the greatest number of people possible in the most direct way," she responded. "And the most direct way is a crusade. He should not let the message be obscured by political overtones or by those well-polished jokes speakers tell at luncheons."

Billy reminded her of the time they had a private dinner at the White House in 1964 with President Lyndon Johnson. The President asked Billy who would make a good Vice-Presidential candidate, at which point Ruth was able to give Billy a warning kick under the table in the family dining room, only to have him blurt out, "Why did you kick me?"

Ruth was embarrassed, but not too embarrassed to remind him, "You're supposed to limit your advice to spiritual matters." The conversation ended abruptly. After dessert, Lady Bird and Ruth preceded their husbands out of the dining room, but Ruth heard the President whisper, "Now that they're gone, what do you think?" Billy, perhaps remembering that kick, changed the subject. Politics dies hard.

Lobbying with politicians for spiritual matters is quite acceptable however. At another dinner in the White House, in 1973 during the visit when Ruth and I had our private talk, she asked my father if there were any way of sending Bibles to all the Americans in foreign prisons. She was especially concerned by news stories about young men and women in foreign hell-holes on drug charges. As a result of her request, the State Department provided the information needed so that the Billy Graham Evangelistic Association could send Bibles to prisons around the world. They are sent in the hope that somehow the Bibles will be delivered to all the prisoners once they arrive.

Billy Graham has ministered to the sick, the poor, the forgotten—and also to the powerful. Every President since World War II has found occasion to call on him, as have many world leaders. Winston Churchill told Graham, "I am without hope for the world." The former Prime Minister was despondent, Billy said, because he believed the world has changed for the worse since he was a boy—with rape and murder, violence and vengeance rampant.

Since Billy Graham has strong ideas about world affairs and especially the course our country is taking I asked the Grahams if it were not a constant temptation for Billy to take an active role in political affairs. He would not be the first minister with a large national following to become involved in politics. Martin Luther King, Jr., had as much political impact as any other figure of the past decades. And despite the traditionalists who believe the primary task of the church is the spiritual salvation of the individual, more and more ministers are seeking public office each year and speaking out on political issues.

I knew that he had been approached several times about running for the Senate and that there were those who would like to see him consider the Presidency.

Ruth Graham, however, is steadfast in her opposition to her husband's involvement in politics. "If he becomes identified with one party or one group, the effort is diminished," she told me. And so Billy, at his wife's urging, has tried to observe a political neutrality.

I realize there are many people who feel that he was not neutral in his relationship with my father during his Presidency. But the close friendship between our families, which dates from 1950, the year my father was elected to the Senate, made a more "correct" distance virtually impossible. It was largely due to my grandmother, Hannah Nixon, that our families became friends. Nana met Billy Graham in 1947 when he was an unknown minister with Youth of Christ. She remembered him and two years later attended the Los Angeles Crusade, which was his first major evangelical effort. A year or so later, my father and Billy were introduced in the Senate dining room by a Democratic senator. My grandmother was the chief subject of their first brief conversation.

Ruth reminds me of Nana more than any woman I have known, though they are quite different in some ways. Nana was shy and reserved; Ruth is sparkling, and can be outrageously funny. Nana was beautiful only to those who knew and loved her; Ruth is a strikingly attractive woman. It seems incongruous to compare Nana with a woman so strongly associated with public displays of belief. My grandmother was so private in her faith that she took the Biblical injunction "When thou prayest, enter into thy closet, and when thou hast shut thy door, pray to thy Father" literally. Except with her sisters, with whom she used the Quaker thee and thou, she rarely spoke about God. When something important was happening in our lives, Nana would say, "I'll be thinking about you," and we knew she meant "I'll be praying for you." But the reason I link Ruth Graham and my grandmother in my mind is that their faith in God—more important to them than anything else in their lives—had made me want to believe also. And like Nana's, Ruth's faith comes from her Bible.

We talked late that night in front of the kitchen fireplace, until the wood was burned down to white ashes. "Let's end the evening in prayer," Billy said. And Ruth, as lithe and quick as a young girl, slipped to her knees. She rested her elbows on the seat of her chair and bowed her head over clasped hands. Billy prayed for those of immediate concern to the three of us, our families and friends, and he prayed for other people, most of whom we would never know or meet —for the starving, the disillusioned, those in prison. As he repeated the familiar verse, "For I was a stranger, and ye took me not in . . . for I was in prison, and ye visited me not . . ." I realized that this was the first time outside of a church that I had ever prayed for someone in jail. Our petitions seemed so enormous I understood why Ruth had instinctively fallen to her knees.

But no matter how enormous the request, for Ruth Graham prayer is "like talking to your best friend," a friend who is by her side twenty-four hours a day. When I had asked Bunny who her mother's best friend was, she seemed puzzled for a moment. She mentioned several people and then said, "I'm not even sure you can say Mother has a best friend, because she doesn't confide in friends that much. Really, the Lord is her best friend." Then Bunny added, as if she felt she had to explain, "I know that is unusual, because most of us—and that includes me—feel we need a human set of ears we can cry or complain to. Even though the Bible teaches us to trust God and to lean on Him."

Ruth never gets very far away from God. When we talked about relaxing on vacations, she told me that she takes three kinds of books on trips—books to inform, books to relax, and a book to serve as a conversation opener "for when I meet someone on the beach." But she relaxes most easily when she reads a psalm or a chapter from the Bible and then, as she sunbathes, memorizes it.

She has always memorized scripture "for the pure joy of it." Her ability to draw on passages from the Bible has often helped her in moments of crisis. A year ago she fell out of a tree while trying to put up a swing and suffered a concussion. She was in pain and terribly confused about dates and events when she eventually regained consciousness. But her greatest distress was her inability to remember the Bible verses she had spent a lifetime learning. For a week, she prayed, "Lord, I can give up anything—but not my Bible verses." It was more than two weeks after her concussion that somewhere from deep within her mind came the words "Yea, I have loved thee with an ever-lasting love: therefore with lovingkindness have I drawn thee." She could not remember what part of the Bible this verse came from and, to this day, she cannot remember when or why she learned this verse from Jeremiah. But as she lay in bed, cherishing these words that had come to her, she knew a sense of great comfort. And she prayed. "Thank you, Lord."

Ruth almost always has a pen and an open notebook beside her when she reads the Bible. Just holding the pen is an act of faith—faith that there will be something new to learn or a passage that relates to what she is feeling or thinking about. She records in her notebooks her reactions to the Bible passages she has studied, and her prayers, too. She puts the date next to every prayer and dates the answers—some immediate, some years later—as well. Not all the answers to her prayers are ones that she originally asked for, but she does not expect to receive everything she asks for. As she told me, quoting the words of the One Hundred and Sixth Psalm, "He gave them their request; but sent leanness into their soul."

Ruth has read and reread six Bibles in her lifetime, studying them until they fell apart from her constant handling. During my visit, she was busy transferring into her seventh King James version some of the notations from the Bible she had studied since 1959. There is a beautiful view of the mountains from the bedroom, but Ruth's study corner there is arranged so that she faces the wall when she works. Every existing English translation of the Bible is on a shelf above her desk. The desk itself is covered with pens, pencils and Ruth's notebooks. I asked her about a small stone on one corner. It seemed out of place. She told me that she had picked it up through the fence that separates Hong Kong from mainland China. It is a constant reminder to her to pray for people living in the country where she was born. Ruth would like to return to

China, especially to visit her infant brother's grave, but she has been unable to obtain a visa. She believes there is a small, but strong, underground Christian church in China and her greatest comfort is to know that off North Korea, on Chedujo Island, the Bible is being transmitted via radio to China. Verses are read at dictation speed so that those listening can copy the scripture and pass it on to others.

Whenever she stops her Bible reading or other work and looks up, the first thing her eyes rest on is a crown of thorns hanging from a nail pounded into the rough log wall. When she was in Jerusalem a few years ago, the Moslem policeman who was acting as her guide cut a branch from a thorny bush beside the dusty road and shaped it into a crown. Ruth believes that Christ's crown of thorns came from the same kind of bush.

Having time to spend in her study corner is a recent luxury for Ruth. When Dr. Graham learned we had been in her work corner, he told me, still starry-eyed in his praise of his wife after thirty-three years together, that for most of their married life Ruth would get up at five in the morning and study her Bible before the children were awake. Ruth, slightly embarrassed, corrected him gently. "Honey, you know how many nights I would be up three to six times with the kids and then I couldn't get up early the next morning." Those days, when all five children were still at home, when she was too tired to get up early and study, she would place the Bible on the kitchen counter and read a verse or two whenever she had a minute. And Bunny remembers going into Ruth's room many times late at night when she was a little girl after waking up from a bad dream and finding her mother on her knees, her elbows resting on the bed, her head bent down in prayer.

I asked Ruth how much time she spends praying every day. She did not answer for a moment, then she said, "It's just a continual conversation. And I'm so glad you don't have to be on your knees to pray. I'd be plain uncomfortable. My knees are knobby."

I understood what she meant by "continual conversation" later on Saturday afternoon when the three of us were sitting on the deck porch off their living room, Billy in a bright sky-blue rocking chair that matched the color of his eyes; Ruth in her favorite unpainted oak rocking chair. She belonged in that chair. Her fresh beauty was as natural as the wood of the chair, burnished from many years of use. Billy read to us from a book on prayer by E. Stanley Jones, Mahatma Gandhi's closest spiritual friend in the Western world. When he finished and we had discussed what he had read—and many other things—Billy offered a short prayer. Ruth bowed her head, but did not get up from her chair to kneel. In the presence of good friends, with the pine-covered valley stretching out below us, it was easy to feel grateful to God. Praying seemed as natural as our conversation had been.

Ruth's approach to her religion is very personal. She is close to God, close to the Bible. "I have learned that there is no keener suffering," she told me, "than to see your children suffer." And she went on to relate this to what God must have felt for his Son on the cross at Calvary. In the same way, she is convinced that "There is no problem a mother faces that Christ does not know already first-hand." Because Joseph is not mentioned after the incident at the temple in Jerusalem, Ruth believes that he died when Jesus was still a boy and that is why Christ postponed his public ministry until his late twenties. Mary needed Him to help care for His seven brothers and sisters. And so, Jesus knew the difficulties and pressures of rearing children—the squabbling, the bruised feelings, the frustrations.

Ruth has her own child-rearing philosophy—based on common sense and the Bible. To her way of thinking, the Book of Proverbs has more wisdom than any book on child care she has ever read.

"How can you do better than 'Train up a child in the way he should go: and when he is old, he will not depart from it?" she asks.

She trusts God so completely that she can let go of her worries about her children and even resist the natural temptation to cling. If you cannot fulfill your own concept of perfection, she says, why try to make your children fit into a perfect mold. A friend of thirty years told me, "Ruth has cherished the freedom of being herself. She is allowed to be Ruth. And so she does not try to control or mold those she loves." And it is true. She is herself. Ruth Bell Graham, not only Mrs. Billy Graham. In return, Ruth has allowed her children to be themselves whether their choice was fashion modeling or college dropout. Several of her children told me that they will always be grateful to their parents for never once telling them that "you can't do that or say that, because of the ministry." Not surprisingly, the five children are markedly independent and all three of her daughters made their own decisions about marriage at an early age.

The Grahams' elder son Franklin was the child who most tempted them to intervene. It took Franklin almost seven years to complete four years of college. There were always other things he wanted to do including helping build a hospital in Jerusalem. When he finally finished the two-year college in Montreat, his cousin graduated the same day with honors. But Ruth can laugh as she quotes her son, "I just graduated with relief."

Franklin grew up in the happy environment of the log house on top of the mountain, but he did not have an easy childhood. It may be even more difficult to be a minister's son than the child of a politician. Not only did Franklin have to establish his own identity, but also he faced enormous pressure to resolve his own spiritual questions as if he were a carbon copy of his father. Franklin was the only Graham child who, though he joined the family prayers, was silent about his own beliefs.

Shortly after Franklin was born, Ruth wrote, "Spiritual growth can't be forced without raising a little brood of hypocrites." The children prayed at least once a day with their parents, usually after breakfast. They were never taught specific prayers, but encouraged to "talk to God in their own way." Sunday was the special family day. There was always some kind of shared activity or outing in the afternoon and the children were given treats that were forbidden on other days, like candy or Cokes. It was the Lord's day, a day to rejoice and be grateful.

But Billy was not home most Sundays when the children were young. He was gone at least nine months of the year—in Hong Kong or Nairobi or Chicago. Both the Grahams now feel that his absences were especially difficult for their sons, even though Ruth was strong and not a coddling or overprotective mother. She encouraged all her children to be independent and nurtured their sense of adventure.

Franklin started "camping out" by himself when he was five. Ruth told me the story of his first night out— on the front porch. In the morning she asked him if he hadn't been worried that the polecat might come around.

"No ma'am," Franklin answered.

"Why not?"

"I had my gun with me."

"Honey, that wasn't a real gun."

"Oh, Mom, the polecat didn't know that!"

The top floor of the house was the children's domain. Billy told me that he never entered any of the children's rooms without an invitation. The second floor was simply off limits for adults except when Ruth made an inspection tour. And that was not often. She is easy-going about house cleaning. During my visit, the Grahams' cat did not make a single appearance all weekend. He does not like Yro and dislikes company even more. Now that the children are gone the cat has claimed their floor as his own. Ruth told me she is fighting a losing battle with the cat hairs. But she did not seem concerned.

In those early years Ruth carried most of the burden of discipline and in retrospect feels that she was not strict enough. She worries that in compensating for the children missing their father so much she loved them "not wisely but too well." But she never hesitated to spank them. She believed the advice offered in Proverbs: "Foolishness is bound in the heart of a child; but the rod of correction shall drive it far from him." Often she would spank two or three times a day, if necessary. Gigi, her eldest daughter, whom Ruth describes as "a real humdinger," came in for the greatest number of spankings. The amount of attention Gigi was getting finally galvanized her five-year-old sister, Bunny, into action. She was naughty for three days in a row. In exasperation, Ruth finally spanked her. Bunny was very pleased with herself. "When you spank me it means you love me," she told Ruth.

Today, Gigi has five children. Recently she worried about how much of her day she spent yelling at her children. She asked her mother, "Why is it that you never screamed at us?" Ruth answered, "You just don't remember, I did all the time." She told Gigi that one night she was terribly discouraged because she had scolded them all day. In exhaustion, she turned to God and prayed, "Please don't let the children remember this." Perhaps her prayer has been answered. Three of the children told me that while they clearly remember the spankings, they have no memory of Ruth constantly screaming.

When the children reached age thirteen or so, Ruth tried to learn to listen rather than reprimand. "I found that sometimes when they shocked me the most, they were just using me as a sounding board." Ruth expressed strong opinions on moral issues only. Long hair, beards, jeans—all were familiar sights around the Graham house and no cause for lectures.

Her trust in her children and in God did not fail her, even with the son who seemed spiritually so far away. After his wedding ceremony held on the lawn at the Graham house, twenty-one-year-old Franklin surprised his parents and friends by announcing that he and his bride had decided to commit their lives to God's service. For Ruth and Billy, it had been a long journey.

Ruth Graham chose to have five children. Both the Grahams are convinced that a mother's job is the "hardest and most important job in the world." Ruth believes that the real liberation mothers need is to be freed from the burden of working outside the home. She does not believe motherhood can be a part-time job. "A mother, like God, must be a very present help in time of trouble," she told me. "Children do not wait until five-thirty in the afternoon to encounter a problem."

"But what about women who have to work?" I asked.

She had a ready answer. "Children are perceptive," she said, "They know if their mother is working for an extra color television or because the family cannot do without the money she earns."

"What about those women who feel they do not have the patience to stay home all day long with small children?"

Ruth unblinkingly said, "I believe one can learn to be patient."

One almost has to be sitting next to Ruth as I was when she expresses these opinions. Otherwise she sounds rigid and, given the aspirations of women today, unrealistic. But when she describes being a mother, she is so earnest. She does not feel she denied herself during the years she spent with her children. She looks at a woman's life as a matter of timing—

with different roles at different stages. Today, now that her children are grown, she has time for the poetry, painting and sewing she enjoys. She has the freedom to travel with her husband. As she talked, I was more aware than I had been before that her tanned face, although still youthful, is deeply lined. The lines seemed evidence of the struggle of bearing and almost single-handedly raising five children. But it was a struggle that Ruth clearly gloried in. I sensed no hint of regret.

Ruth feels there is no institution more worth fighting for than the family. The fight is difficult because the parents, two completely different people, must try to function as a single unit. In the words of the Bible, man and wife become "one flesh." Ruth describes marriage as a triangle: God at the top, with husband and wife on the same plane on the bottom. While the husband has certain responsibilities in the home and, in Ruth's view, final authority, and the wife other responsibilities, marriage is not a question of lording it over each other, it is a question of giving in to each other.

Ruth and Billy Graham have not found marriage to be an easy merger. A different culture, a different outlook on the world and different challenges separated Ruth Bell from Billy Graham. She grew up as a missionary's child in China, he on a dairy farm in North Carolina. Only one thing brought them together —their faith in God.

Ruth's childhood was spent in the Chinese village of Tsing-kiangpu, where her medical missionary parents had established a three-hundred-and-eighty-bed hospital. From the time she was a baby, Ruth was familiar with death and suffering. She remembers the day she saw a pack of dogs devouring a baby, abandoned because it was a girl. It was a harsh life. There were nights when Ruth's mother would be awakened by her children's screams of terror—rats were crawling over their beds. Bubonic plague and other diseases were rampant. Death was a very real presence. Not only death from disease. They lived in bandit country and every night some three hundred people were captured—some tortured, some killed. "I don't believe I ever went to sleep without hearing the sound of gunshots," she said. During the conflict between the Japanese and Chinese in the late 1930s, Ruth became accustomed to Japanese bombers flying over the house—so low she could see the bombs in the bomb racks. Today her daughter Gigi says, "Mother just doesn't know what it means to be afraid."

Ruth grew up seeing the people she loved most—her parents and her Chinese nanny—read the Bible daily. The nanny, Wang Nai Nai, who took care of Ruth and her two sisters and brothers, had been a procuress before her conversion. As an old woman she had taught herself to read so that she could read her own Bible. Because Ruth lived among many Chinese like her nurse, whose lives had been changed as a result of their Christian conversion, her faith in God was unlimited, and, until she went away to boarding school in North Korea, untested.

She was only thirteen and so homesick for her family that she cried herself to sleep for three weeks. She felt lost spiritually as well. "I knew Christ had died for the whole world," Ruth told me, "but who was I among so many?" Finally, she was sent to the infirmary. "I lay there in bed and for an entire afternoon I read the Psalms. I just drank them in." Then she turned to the Book of John. In the sixteenth verse of the third chapter she read, "For God so loved the world, that he gave his only begotten Son, that whosoever believeth in him should not perish, but have everlasting life." Hundreds of times before she had read the words or heard her parents recite them, but for the first time she believed they applied to her. She wrote her name next to the verse and claimed it as a truth in her own life.

It is not surprising that what she remembers most

about meeting Billy Graham when they were students at Wheaton College is that "he wanted to please God more than any man I'd ever met." Billy had sought Ruth out because he had heard there was a girl on campus so devout she got up at five every morning to pray. When he met Ruth, he learned that the campus gossip was true—give or take an hour depending upon whether or not Ruth had been out on a late date the night before. He also discovered that she was a beautiful girl, with eyes more gold than hazel, long dark lashes, and a good figure. "I fell in love with Ruth the minute I saw her," Billy told me.

But it took a year before Ruth agreed to marry him. The main stumbling block in Billy's courtship was his previous engagement. He had been deeply hurt when the girl he had loved and planned to marry changed her mind at the last minute and decided to marry someone else. He promised himself that he would never kiss a girl again unless he was engaged to her. "I guess I was guarding against getting hurt a second time," he said. But Ruth found his coolness disconcerting. "I wondered what the matter was with him!" she said.

They were married immediately after Ruth graduated. Their early years were a tremendous struggle financially. And then there were all the little differences to contend with. Both learned to appreciate Ruth's favorite saying—"A happy marriage is the union of two forgivers." Billy is consistently punctual; Ruth tries to be. Billy is well-organized; Ruth's desk is a happy disarray of notes and letters. Billy takes naps as a way of lessening the daily pressures of his life; Ruth never naps.

The most difficult adjustment for Ruth in the early years of their marriage was learning to live with a man who had grown up in a family where the women did not take much part in the conversation. "In my family, women were very outspoken," Ruth said. "I had to learn with Bill that when I spoke, I should speak with more wisdom.

"My home life was so different," she added. "We were missionaries so we had to depend upon each other for company. In the evenings we took turns reading through the classics. Bill was more of a country boy."

There was something else about Ruth that Billy would learn later. She not only was used to speaking up and joining in the conversation, but also she had the kind of steely will that enabled her to resist the pressure from his family and friends who insisted that the Graham children be raised as Baptists. "They were not raised as Baptists. Or Presbyterians," Ruth told me. "They were raised as Christians." She was strong enough to keep her own identity, even as Billy was becoming more and more famous and as her life became more and more entwined with the team members who surround her husband. Grady Wilson (the brother of another Graham aide, T. W. Wilson) is Billy's usual traveling companion. He loves to tease. He is also a compulsive organizer. Several years ago when the team was flying from Albuquerque, New Mexico, to Japan for a crusade, Grady announced that he would give everyone a sleeping pill so that they could sleep during the long flight. Ruth, seeing a golden opportunity to tease Grady—and possibly having had enough of being organized—bought some empty pill capsules and filled them with powdered mustard. She substituted her mustard pills for Grady's sleeping pills—warning everyone else of what she had done. The following morning Grady complained he had just spent "the worst night of my life." Despite a double dose of pills, he did not sleep all night. And had heartburn to boot.

Ruth and I were sitting in the living room after lunch on Sunday as she reminisced about her childhood and the early years of her marriage. It was a beautiful room with its hand-hewn log walls, the flowers and greenery from her garden which Ruth had arranged, the view of the mist-covered valley below. We were in front of the fire. It was raining and we needed the fire to take the damp chill off the room. Ruth apologized for the rain, but when I told her that I had always liked the sound of the rain and the feel of it on my face, she smiled and said, "I always associate rain with happy times. When I was little, we would read and play games on rainy days. But Bill hates the rain. It sends his blood pressure up at least ten points. The sun seems to help him." After a moment, she said, "Bill doesn't like it here in Montreat for more than a week or so at a time these days, because it rains so much."

I thought of how much Ruth loved this house where her children had grown up and of all the beauty she had created in it. I realized that Ruth was still making adjustments in her marriage and that even now she was learning to accept her husband's reluctance to live the quiet round-the-hearth retirement life that she perhaps once thought possible. A lifetime of travel, a constant succession of new faces and places, had made it difficult for Billy Graham to settle down peacefully.

We had gone to church that morning in the Presbyterian Chapel in Montreat where the Grahams had been married. In an effort to worship unnoticed, we sat in the last row of the crowded church. The mica in its stone walls gleams as if it were diamonds and gives this chapel, hidden away in the Black Mountains, a romantic beauty. The Grahams are famous now, their lives very different from anything they had dreamed of when they were married in the chapel, but the love between them is still as enduring as the mica in its walls. It was evident from the moment I arrived in Montreat until they drove me to the airport last Sunday afternoon. As we said good-bye, I was glad that the Grahams would have a few hours to themselves before Billy left for his next trip on Monday. They were planning to stop at a McDonald's on

76

the way home for hamburgers and Billy had made an effort to disguise himself with a plaid hat and dark glasses.

Ten years after their wedding, Ruth wrote a poem about her husband. Not about the Billy Graham the public knows, but about the Bill (as she always calls him) she chose to share her life with:

> I met you years ago
> when
> of all the men
> I knew,
> you,
> I hero-worshipped
> then;
> you are my husband now . . .
> and from my home—
> your arms—
> I turn to look
> down the long trail of years
> to where I met you first
> and hero-worshipped,
> and I would smile;
> . . . I know you better now:
> the faults,
> the odd preferments,
> the differences
> that make you *you*.
>
> That other me—
> so young,
> so far away—
> saw you
> and hero-worshipped
> but never *knew*,
> while I,
> grown wiser
> with the closeness of these years,
> hero-worship, too!

I thanked her for showing her poem to me. "I would write the same thing again today," she said.

Ruth's life has revolved around her husband. It is the life she has chosen for herself. Her marriage is based on a perceptive understanding of the limits of the institution and of human nature. Not too long ago, she wrote down her philosophy for her daughters and other women. "Don't expect your husband to be what only Jesus Himself can be. . . . Don't expect him to give you the security, the joy, the peace, the love that only God Himself can give you."

Ruth has practiced this particular preaching all her married life. Her daughter Bunny told me how, during a Christmas visit home a few years ago, she had stormed into her father's room, because she and her husband of a few weeks had had their first big fight. Her father was obviously reluctant to interfere and told Bunny that he really felt helpless when it came to giving advice. "Your mother and I had our differences when we were first married," he said, "but I learned early that she was married to the Lord first."

The truth is that Ruth never intended to marry. When she met Billy, she fell in love, but she still did not want to give up her dream of becoming a missionary like her parents. Years later, she wrote a poem that revealed the depth of her dilemma and how, after prayer, she resolved the problem of her conflicting desires.

> My heart will not give in.
> We gave in,
> My heart and I.

I found it difficult to understand her youthful desire to spend her life as "an old maid missionary or a martyr in Tibet or some frontier country." I was particularly curious about her desire for martyrdom. Ruth, quite openly and seriously, said, "When I was a girl, I was always in awe of those who offered the greatest gift of all, their lives, in their eagerness to serve God." She does not regret, however, her decision to marry. "I have come to realize there are other ways to serve Him, and I understand the words 'the long martyrdom of life' now.

"I couldn't have made it down through the years without the knowledge that the Lord Jesus was with me," she said simply.

She could not have endured the long separations from her husband, the nights she would go to bed with his old, rough sports coat because she missed him so desperately. Nor could she have learned to accept the chronic cough that has beset her for the last fifteen years. It is only recently that the Mayo Clinic arrived at a tentative diagnosis. The doctors there now believe that it is caused by raw nerve endings in her throat. Whatever the cause, the persistent hacking often kept Ruth—and Billy—awake until dawn. Finally she was forced to move into a bedroom which adjoins his. These days she teases Billy—and only half in jest—that the next gossip about the Grahams will be the "real" reason they sleep in separate bedrooms. And her faith has enabled Ruth to accept without bitterness the knowledge that few people will ever understand the strain of being a public person, or understand just how much her husband has given up by not seeing more of his children as they grew to maturity.

How many times over the years did the children kiss their father good-bye as he left on one of his trips? And how many times did they watch Ruth say good-bye to their father? It was always a brief farewell. Ruth would walk quickly out to the car in the driveway with Billy, help him load the last items into the trunk and give him a quick kiss—more of a peck than a kiss, as if any intimacy would make the moment even more difficult. She would go back into the house immediately after Billy had driven off. "Let's look forward to his coming back," she would tell the children, usually adding, "We have to learn to make the least of all that goes and the most of all that comes." And she would immediately begin a major project in preparation for Billy's homecoming—spring cleaning, refinishing furniture and, more often than not, studying something completely new. During one three-month absence, she read all the fiction of Dostoevsky and Tolstoy and their biographies so that she would have something new to share when Billy came home. And always, Ruth read her Bible and wrote poetry. Only in her poems and to God did she confide the moments of loneliness the children never saw.

It is the knowledge that she is a partner in her husband's ministry that has sustained Ruth Graham more than anything else. Her desire to serve God is unquenchable. Like the Biblical Ruth, it is the very essence of her life.

The words of Ruth's most beloved hymn promise, "Thou art coming to a King/Large petitions with thee bring/For His grace and power are such/None can ever ask too much." If, as the Grahams devoutly believe, the Lord has given Billy the gift of evangelism, Ruth has been given the gift of faith. Like a quiet stream, it runs deliberately and very deep. It is the center of her life. It touches the lives of all those who cross her path.

Charles,
Prince
of
Wales

"The older I get, the more alone
I become."

"LET'S RUN down the stairs."

It was the end of the future King of England's first day in the United States, July 16, 1970, and we were at the top of the Washington Monument, the last stop on a sightseeing tour of Washington landmarks by night. The sultry miasma rising from the land that had once been swamp obscured the view and twenty-one-year-old Prince Charles, who had already devoted untold hundreds of hours of his life to monument inspections, turned away from the viewing rail after a courteous few moments and casually made his suggestion.

It was directed to no one in particular; certainly not to the press "pool" of four reporters who hovered near us to record the Prince's impressions of Washington. There was a stunned silence and then weak smiles at the thought of the hot, grimy stairwell only a few feet away. Princess Anne and I exchanged strained glances.

Charles confidently moved toward the door marked EXIT. "Let's go," he said. And with that, the Prince of Wales started running down the 555 steps of the monument. My husband David, with the quick reflex action of a good host, was right behind him.

Without a word, the Princess, my sister Tricia and I stepped into the elevator. As we began our descent we could hear them pounding down the stairs. "Let's race them," I said in a weak attempt to enter the spirit of the occasion. Through the narrow elevator window we caught glimpses of Prince Charles in his expensive suit that looked as if it had been sculpted to his body, his white cuffs gleaming and every strand of his rigidly parted hair still in place, streaking past. He kept pace with us almost all the way down and burst into the lobby seconds after we stepped out of the elevator. David was a full flight of stairs behind him. And then his fortyish equerry David Chequetts, his Scotland Yard detective, and the clutch of Secret Service agents who had fallen in behind the Prince and David came hurtling, red-faced and perspiring, down the last steps.

The agents looked distraught. I knew how meticulously they had surveyed all the monuments we were scheduled to visit that night, located every exit, determined how close the nearest hospital was and the fastest route to it, prepared for all eventualities except one —that our royal visitor would run down the stairs of the Washington Monument.

When we got back into the large black Presidential limousine, I glanced at the Prince. Apart from a slight pink glow, he appeared as cool and well-groomed as he had been before the race down the monument stairs.

The downstairs sprint was not to be forgotten easily. Every time David stepped off a curb, got out of the car or climbed stairs the next day, he winced. I discovered that there were many in the press corps—and in the official party as well—who wondered if the Prince's action was to show he could be unpredictable even in the midst of a rigidly programmed, international goodwill tour. The business of being a "royal" is a very serious business indeed, and the rigidities extend to the most minute details. For instance, each time we used the car during the three-day visit, we were positioned according to the seating chart that had been given us—the Prince on the right, the Princess on the left, Tricia in the middle and David and I on jump seats in front of them.

At times throughout the visit I was embarrassed to

find myself in the ranks of royalty-watchers and second-guessers. My sister and I had been the object of a similar kind of scrutiny for several years at that point and we disliked it. We were uncomfortable having our private lives made so public. But Tricia and I could remind each other that our day in the public eye was limited. And the interest in us did not begin to compare with that in Charles. Every act, every opinion, indeed every emotion he had displayed from babyhood was and is and will be analyzed in view of his future as King of England.

For Charles is a prince in a kingdom that no longer needs princes—or kings. He is a media personality in a world so inundated by media personalities that despite all royal caution and precaution, the image of the Prince of Wales is almost inevitably tarnished by association. He has lived with merciless publicity all his life. It is part of his "job" as Prince of Wales, and much of the publicity is palace-authorized in an attempt to satisfy public interest. He must be seen, and his activities described. He must submit to press coverage and at the same time repel as best he can the grosser intrusions into his private life. But he is almost powerless to control the degree of exposure. So great was the interest in one "romance" that ten thousand people descended upon the village of Sandringham and crowded around the little church to see Charles and the young woman he was dating attend Sunday services.

Almost everyday of his life Charles has to draw the line mentally on what he will allow to be quoted and what not. He must cope with such questions as, "Do you wear pajamas to bed?" And his very refusal to answer that inquiry became a story in itself. The amount of attention given even the most trivial of his public utterances frequently verges on the ridiculous. When he planted an oak, remarking that he was glad it was not "one of those ghastly spruces," the spruce-lovers of the nation raised their voices in protest. His comments on women's liberation, marriage, political protestors, on anything at all, tend all to often to come back to haunt him. This imposes tremendous pressures. He must always express the "correct" views because, as he has learned, "I'm then held to those views for the rest of my life virtually."

Because of this pressure from the world about him and equal pressure from within himself, Charles has come to tolerate—and probably accept—most of the realities of royal birth, including the periodic rumblings about the high cost of the monarchy. Charles lives in a 115-room mansion on an estate valued at one million pounds. His annual salary is half a million pounds, augmented by revenues from the Duchy of Cornwall that come to more than a million and a quarter pounds a year in addition to the Duchy's traditional payment of two greyhounds, a pound of pepper, a hunting bow, gilt spurs, firewood, a pound of herbs, a gray cloak, one hundred old shillings, a large salmon, and a pair of gloves, all of which are presented with appropriate pagentry each year. With such wealth Charles probably will never be free of the feeling that he is indebted to the public and therefore at their command.

"I am constantly feeling I have to justify myself and my existence," Charles has said. "I must set an example. I must show people I am prepared to do things that they are expected to do." Charles insists that the greatest compliment anyone can pay him is to say, "He's so ordinary." The poignance of his desire reveals a great deal about the young man who, for the rest of his life, must be forever conscious of his public image. Although he protests, "I couldn't care less about my image," the world will make him care. He cannot escape the truth of André Gide's observation that "We make a man become what we think of him."

Many images of Charles had floated through my mind as my mother and Tricia and I prepared for the royal visit. Charles as a solemn infant with sleepy eyes, almost hidden by the satin bows of the fragile, beautifully stitched christening gown with its long train in which generations of royal babies had been christened. Charles at three, dressed for his mother's coronation with a full-lace jabot at his throat. Charles at nine, a wispy figure in a doorway at Buckingham Palace, seeming to wear an eerily gigantic crown—the great chandelier in the reception room beyond. And Charles at nineteen, a dark-haired young man kneeling at his mother's feet at Caernarvon Castle in Wales as he swore, "I, Charles, do become your liege man of earthly worship, and faith and truth I will bear unto you to live and die against all manner of folks."

I found the solemn promise of his vow beautifully moving. As Prince of Wales, Charles has a purpose in life, a mission, a mystical obligation. Viewed in its most creative light, to be Prince of Wales can mean a lifetime of service for others. But it is his destiny, not his choice. And it is a life in which the way people perceive him and his efforts becomes much more important than what he actually accomplishes.

His three-day visit to the United States with his nineteen-year-old sister, Princess Anne, gave Americans an opportunity to see Charles in action, to observe the person who said with refreshing candor, "I used to be shy, but I got over it through the sheer fact of trying."

The visit was designed so he would not "miss anything," and the program that faced him was truly grueling. As the British Embassy kept adding new events, Tricia and I started to question some of the additions. Each time we were assured that "This is something their Royal Highnesses are particularly interested in." In its final form the schedule for the visit included:

A tour of the White House
A helicopter trip to Camp David to have dinner
    with twenty young people

A nighttime tour of the Washington Monument and the Lincoln and Jefferson Memorials

A ceremonial visit to the House of Representatives and to the Senate

An inspection of the space exhibit at the Smithsonian

A luncheon and boat trip to Mount Vernon followed by a tour of George Washington's home

A dinner dance at the White House for six hundred people

A tour of Georgetown

A tour of the Patuxent Wildlife Center

A baseball game

A visit to the Phillips Art Gallery

Tea at the British Embassy

A private conversation with the President

An intimate dinner—just family—at the White House

And all this within fifty-three hours. This heavy scheduling was not all that unusual, at least not for the British royal family. David's grandfather had commented indignantly on a similar brutal program arranged for Charles' parents thirteen years earlier. "I told Prime Minister Macmillan," President Eisenhower said, "that I would have fired any aide who dared to set up a program like theirs for me." But Prince Charles is forever fated to be in the position of "not missing anything" whenever and wherever he goes on a royal tour. I doubt that he will ever protest, because he is a conscientious person, extremely aware of his royal duties.

I had swallowed the assurances of the British Embassy that Prince Charles and Princess Anne were intensely interested in each scheduled event, even though I myself had been the victim in the past of overly ambitious scheduling. Consequently, my astonishment was painfully real when on the last day of their tour, after the Prince had been taken to observe birds in a wildlife sanctuary and after he had sweltered in ninety-three-degree weather at a baffling and boring baseball game, he whispered with some apprehension as we started our visit to the Phillips Gallery, "We aren't going to have a long tour here, are we?"

Tricia and I particularly had questioned this addition to the program. But we had been told that the Prince of Wales was very fond of the work of the French Impressionists and most eager to see paintings at the Phillips. My suspicions about the Prince's control of his schedule were doubly confirmed later when I came across an interview he had given some months before his visit, in which he had made a point of saying that he had absolutely no interest in baseball nor any particular desire to see a baseball game.

The royal visit became a major media event from the moment it was announced a full month before Charles and Anne were due to arrive in Washington. The press learned, for instance, that no reporters would be allowed to cover his visit with Speaker of the House John McCormack. There would be an opportunity to take photographs, but the writing press would be barred. Speaker McCormack had felt that the Prince would be more at ease in asking questions about the workings of the American government and that both could speak more freely if the press were not recording every word. But his thoughtfulness stirred up a hornet's nest.

At the White House briefing, the journalists told my mother's press secretary, Constance Stuart, "You ought not to put up with that. Little John Monihan [the Speaker's aide who had given notice of this restriction was the target of their anger] making a decision like that is ridiculous. We want to know what the Speaker says to him [Charles] and what he says to the Speaker." As if Constance Stuart, a member of the White House staff, could countermand Speaker McCormack's arrangements.

Because of a combination of the close press scrutiny, the painstaking precision planning that was necessary if the schedule was to work and, most of all, the prerequisite that everyone "have a good time," there was considerable tension before the Prince and Princess arrived. The attention paid to every detail was truly staggering. The British Embassy briefed us, for instance, that Her Royal Highness would wear a hat during the formal welcoming ceremony on the White House lawn, although we were not prepared for her three-quarter-length gloves nor for the soft felt hat that the Prince of Wales, who was dressed entirely in chocolate brown from his shoes to the hat, carried in the ninety-degree heat.

The ceremony that surrounded them—the curtsies, the "Your Royal Highnesses," the "Sirs" and the "Ma'ams" that accompanied every meeting and every conversation—was difficult to adjust to. It was strained for me and many of my friends to address someone our own age so formally as "Your Royal Highness." Fortunately I found that when I wanted to speak to Charles or Anne, I was always able to catch his or her eye, so that I succeeded in sidestepping the problem altogether.

I was not the only one to be slightly ill at ease with all the formality. Even the senior members of the White House domestic staff felt its effect, although many of them remembered Queen Elizabeth's 1957 visit. The third floor, where the six small guest rooms were and where David and I stayed when we visited the White House, was almost spookily quiet during the royal visit. There was none of the customary laughter and chatter in the red-carpeted halls. The staff seemed to be in awe of the Prince's valet and Princess Anne's personal maid, who were staying on the third floor. The Britishers did not mingle with the White House maids and ushers. All their meals were served to them in their own sitting rooms including, as one of the maids told me, with respectful wonder, tea, complete with toast and little cakes and pastries, twice a day.

There was no resentment of their requirements or of the air of decorum that had descended upon the third floor. Quite the opposite. The staff was intensely interested in every aspect of our visitor's lives. One morning the Princess's maid wanted to do some ironing, so the maid on duty excitedly set up the ironing board and even put some fresh flowers in the laundry room for her. The Princess's maid started ironing one of her own dresses. "Aren't you going to iron anything for the Princess?" the White House maid asked. "Oh no," was the reply. "My Princess gives me very little to do." The White House maid, who had thought she was going to watch one of the Princess's dresses being ironed, was crushed.

I felt the royal presence as well. Several times I caught myself starting down the back stairway to the second floor to see my parents or meet the Prince and Princess—and stopped just in time. For the duration of the visit that stairway and the East Hall it opened onto below were British territory. The East Hall's heavy oak sliding doors had been closed to provide a living room for our royal guests. I had to remember to take the elevator at the other end of the hall. It was not a major adjustment, just a reminder that even the White House is not so large that the presence of guests goes unnoticed.

Slightly more unsettling was the fact that the Prince's valet, an older man, very quiet and reserved, and quite tiny, almost like an extremely dignified gnome, was in the bedroom directly across the hall from David and me. In the morning I usually would turn off the alarm clock, roll out of bed, take three steps to the door, fling it open and pick up the newspapers. But after a startled, early-morning eye-to-eye confrontation with the valet, I resorted to the long-arm-around-the-door technique to retrieve the papers.

Prince Charles, despite all the formality with which

he was surrounded, always managed to come through as a thoughtful human being, not a royal robot. He had a gift for putting people at ease. In the first few hours of his visit, he charmed twenty of our friends whom we had invited to join us at Camp David for an evening of sports followed by dinner on the terrace. It could have been an awkward occasion since they were all strangers to Charles and Anne, but, in fact, it was almost as if the Prince were the host. He approached everyone with an open friendliness and made an unobtrusive point of talking with each guest. One of our friends, a graduate of a one-room schoolhouse on a Maine island, had been nervous at the prospect of making conversation with the Prince of Wales. But when the two met, the talk was as easy and natural as if they had known each other for years.

The British Embassy had told us that the Prince likes to shoot skeet, so as soon as we arrived at Camp David we bicycled, with Prince Charles leading the way, to the skeet range. The Prince took the first turn and he was so skilled—he did not miss a shot—that no one wanted to follow him.

When we arrived back at the Lodge for supper, we could smell hamburgers and steaks being grilled on the terrace. But Charles took one look at the pool and supper was delayed while he swam a dozen or so laps of the Olympic-size pool in a strong, competent crawl. One girl whispered to me, "I'm used to people being good at some things, but he's good at everything."

Almost an hour later, we sat down to supper on the terrace. It was an informal meal with banana splits for dessert. Charles liked his so much that he asked for a second. By this time we were running very late, and there was still a tour of Washington monuments by night ahead of us. Charles' equerry suggested that we should leave shortly several times, but the Prince did not seem to hear him. Finally the equerry said firmly, "We've got to leave now, Your Royal Highness, or we're going to be too late to keep the schedule." Charles nodded and in minutes we were at the helicopter pad for the trip back to the White House. I think that everyone would have been in favor of canceling this last item on the master plan of events, but the itinerary had been announced and we knew that there would be crowds—and the press—waiting to see Prince Charles and Princess Anne at each stop.

Whatever else they were, Prince Charles and Princess Anne were true professionals as quick-change artists. I had made what I considered a very fast change from slacks to a dress and stockings and David was still putting on his suit jacket as we hurried down the third-floor hall to take the elevator to the second floor. But when the elevator door opened, Prince Charles and Princess Anne were standing there, waiting. Charles was beautifully groomed again, this time in a gray-blue suit, a fresh white handkerchief in his pocket. The Princess's hair was freshly teased higher than ever. Even with a valet and maid to help them, it was an impressive performance.

When we got home well after eleven that night, there was no question of staying up to talk. We were all tired, and the schedule for the next morning called for a nine-thirty departure for Capitol Hill. Tricia, David and I said good-night to our guests on the second floor, where Princess Anne was staying in the Queen's Bedroom suite and Prince Charles in the Lincoln Bedroom.

Normally the Prince and Princess would not have stayed at the White House, but at Blair House, just one block away, where most important foreign visitors and their aides stay. The house, beautifully decorated with American antiques, is large and consequently there is more privacy—and comfort—for visitors there than in the White House. It is their home and their staff for as long as they are in Washington.

But Queen Elizabeth had sent a personal message to my father through Walter Annenberg, the United

States Ambassador to the Court of St. James's. The Queen had asked—quite sentimentally—if her son and daughter could have the same quarters in the White House that she and the Duke of Edinburgh had occupied on their visit to the United States in 1957 and that her mother and father, Queen Elizabeth and King George VI, had occupied in 1939. Of course, the Queen's wish was granted.

I got a glimpse of how strong Charles' sense of history and continuity must be at the arrival ceremony on the South Lawn of the White House when he enthusiastically told my parents and the assembled crowd how much he was looking forward to his stay in the Lincoln Bedroom. "It is a peculiar honor, I think," the Prince said.

Charles, however, could not know that what he called "a peculiar honor" was making my mother quite nervous. He was the first state visitor to use the Lincoln Bedroom since she and my father had been in the White House. It is a rather gloomy room with its heavy, horsehair-covered Victorian furniture. But it does evoke the age of Lincoln and the spirit of the man. There is a copy of the Gettysburg Address in President Lincoln's own hand on the desk. And the eight-foot-one-inch-long bed is the one that Mrs. Lincoln bought for the President more than a century ago, although he never slept in it.

At the time of Prince Charles' visit, I had a feeling that the mattress was almost as old as the bed. It was lumpy and hard, and to me, felt like straw. For at least a year, I had told visitors whom I guided through the White House that it was indeed filled with straw. But when word of this detail of my tour reached the curator, he sent me a short, crisp note advising me formally that the historic bed had a horsehair mattress. My mother was concerned that Prince Charles would be uncomfortable, but since eight-foot-one-inch mattresses are not easy to obtain practically overnight,

94

she had no choice but to leave the old mattress on the bed.

None of us could forget the story of Winston Churchill's stay at the White House during World War II when he was an unhappy occupant of the Lincoln Bedroom. Characteristically, he remedied the situation himself. Near midnight on the first day of his visit, one of the ushers was startled to see the Prime Minister, wearing absolutely nothing but his slippers, a suitcase in each hand, moving himself across the hall to the comforts of the Queen's suite.

The morning after Charles' first night my mother waited anxiously with Tricia, David and me to say hello to the Prince and, she hoped, find out if he had had a good night. As he came down the hall, we all felt relieved. He was swinging his arms briskly as if he were carrying a walking stick. He not only looked rested, but also there was no hint of any morning-after twinges from his run down the Washington Monument only ten hours earlier. Knowing how sore David was, I was amazed Charles showed no signs of stiffness. There was no need to ask his equerry how he felt, however. David Chequetts limped slightly and, no matter how nonchalant he tried to appear, he could not hide his discomfort during the rest of the visit. Charles' first words were to tell my mother what a comfortable night he had had. We were grateful he was such a good sport, but, nevertheless, several months later my mother retired the mattress to the White House archives.

The second day of the visit started off with the ceremonial tours of the House of Representatives and the Senate. After the long, hot climb under the blazing Washington sun to the top of the Capitol steps, escorted and surrounded by officials of the Congress, city police, Capitol police, Secret Service agents and what appeared to be the majority of the Washington press corps, their Royal Highnesses were welcomed by the seventy-nine-year-old Speaker of the House, John

McCormack. As he held Princess Anne's arm in grandfatherly fashion, Anne jerked it away, an act that was caught by the television cameras and duly shown on the news later that day.

Charles noticed his sister's annoyance and whispered to her, "It's much easier coming down," trying to reassure her that the ordeal would soon be over and she would be back in the air-conditioned limousine. The limousine became our refuge as the visit wore on. It was a place to talk and relax. We found that we all shared an enthusiasm for movies. We talked about our travel experiences and quite a bit about conservation, in which Charles was very interested.

At times we fell silent. The strain of so many public appearances, so many introductions, so many conversations with strangers took its toll and we were glad for the peace and quiet of the limousine. Charles would ask, "Now where is it we're going next?" We would tell him and then sit there quietly. Someone might make an occasional remark, but most of the time there was a comfortable silence. Shortly before we were due to arrive, Charles often asked who would be there and then he would fall silent again, preparing himself, thinking about the people he was to meet and what he would say. He was hard-working and appeared to be genuinely interested in all the people he met and the places he visited, even when, as in the case of the Phillips Gallery, I knew that his interest was perfunctory.

This was not true of his sister. The young blond Princess was having an increasingly difficult time feigning interest in the city of Washington. Astronaut Neil Armstrong's description of the moon rock on display at the Smithsonian Institution seemed to interest her mildly, but during her visit to the United States Senate, the Princess, who had informed us that she did not like history when she studied it in school, assumed the "Look straight ahead. Notice nothing to left or right, and you'll be liberated sooner" attitude.

She seemed incapable of handling the interest of the media in her first impressions of Washington. When a reporter asked how she liked the Lincoln Memorial, she responded, "I do not give interviews." Thinking her question had been misunderstood, the reporter repeated it. Anne stonily replied, "I do not talk to the press." By the time Anne pulled her arm away from Speaker McCormack, the media were more than ready to publicize her lack of cooperation and report every observed detail of her distaste for her royal obligations.

Princess Anne's transparently indignant reaction to the American press made it obvious that she never before had been exposed to a situation in which the press could actually approach and ask questions. It was also clear that neither she nor her brother had been briefed on how to handle the American press.

Charles gradually and with good humor mastered this new wrinkle in the public relations aspect of being a prince. He did not unbend enough to give the press any human interest quotations or anecdotes, but he smiled frequently. Princess Anne on the other hand, who seemed to be torn between feeling a lack of attention and heartily disliking the informal attitude of the American reporters, became more and more withdrawn and unapproachable.

When the White House staff assembled to meet the Prince and Princess, Anne strode quickly past the maids and ushers and chefs, bestowing brief nods of recognition. But Charles stopped and said a few words to each one. At this moment, Anne was a classic example of the public figure who has reached her limits of tolerance and patience. She was tired of being nice to people whom she barely knew and whom she would never see again. Tired of forced smiles. Tired of being a ceremonial figure.

No matter what her mood, Charles was unfailingly supportive of his sister, calm and cheerful, even though occasionally she openly expressed her impatience with him as well. There were times when he would stop to talk with people and thus delay our departure for a few moments and Anne, by her comments, would let him know that it irritated her to have to wait for him. It was a typical sisterly reaction—and would have gone unnoticed with any other brother and sister. But this was the Prince of Wales, the future King, and this was his sister. And the whole of Washington seemed fascinated by their every expression, word and gesture.

During private moments in the course of the visit, however, the Prince and Princess sought out each other's company. Both mornings they requested breakfast together instead of alone in the private sitting rooms off their bedrooms. But as each hour of their stay passed, I wondered more and more why Charles and his sister had traveled to Washington together. She could not conceal her dislike for playing a supporting role, having more attention showered on her brother than on herself.

It was the Prince who spoke at the official welcome on the South Lawn of the White House. It was the Prince whose views and remarks were listened to almost reverently. It was the Prince who had a long private talk with my father in the Oval Office. And it was the Prince who was the more compelling character. He naturally and gracefully stepped to center stage at every stop, at every event, in every gathering.

After the tour of the Capitol, we were joined by another group of young friends for a cruise down the Potomac River to Mount Vernon on the Presidential yacht *Sequoia*. In the planning stages it had seemed like an inspired idea: a pleasant trip on the water, beautiful scenery, an historic destination, a chance to have lunch outdoors and talk informally with young Americans. In truth, it was a mini-disaster.

It was a hot and muggy day, even muggier on the river, and I have never before or since seen the Potomac a deeper shade of murky brown. Dead fish bobbed on its polluted surface. Twenty minutes before we were due to dock at George Washington's estate, Princess Anne disappeared. Suddenly we spotted her at the wheel of one of the Coast Guard speedboats that were escorting us. Her lady-in-waiting—teased and laquered hairdo disintegrating in the spray—was huddled in the stern as the boat roared by. The Princess rejoined us at the Mount Vernon dock. She gave no explanation. We asked no questions.

There was a time when I felt the Princess was truly enjoying herself and that was the evening of the ball. The receiving line was headed by Tricia. Charles stood next to her and I stood between Charles and Anne so that I could introduce the guests to her. But many people, in the excitement of meeting the Prince of Wales and his sister, assumed that the girl next to the Prince must be the Princess. Curtsies and "Your Royal Highnesses" were generously bestowed upon me. Anne and I tried to suppress our laughter, but there were times when it was impossible. Finally I said, "We'd better change places." "Oh, no," Anne replied with a devilish smile, "I'm rather enjoying this." And she really was.

I, not Tricia, had the first dance with Prince Charles that evening. There was a reason. My sister was embarrassed by rumors and news stories of a romance between her and Prince Charles, especially since she and Edward Cox, whom she married a year later, were secretly engaged at the time. We thought that if Tricia had the first dance with Charles, it might increase the speculation. So while David danced with Princess Anne, I danced with Prince Charles—at arm's length. He was very pleasant, commented on the music, which was purposely slow and nondescript so that even those who could do only the two-step shuffle would be encouraged to join us on the floor for the first dance. But his attention was elsewhere. He seemed miles away. Actually, very guardedly, he was already looking for someone, somewhere on that

crowded dance floor, to have fun with that evening. I
hoped he was successful. Everything was so beautiful
that night, it seemed as if all the guests, and especially the guest of honor, should have a good time. A
tent formed by thousands of tiny glittering lights had
been erected over the dance floor on the White House
lawn. And one could look up through the lights and
see the full July moon in the sky above.

But Charles need not have bothered to scan the
pretty faces at the ball. During the third dance of the
evening, his partner felt a tap on her shoulder—and
suddenly the Prince was dancing with someone who
had chosen him. He concealed his astonishment mas-
terfully, but when he came back to where we were sitting he could not resist telling us that it was the first
time in his life a woman had ever asked him to dance.
It was not the last. Charles kept finding his partners
switched with the result that he spent quite a bit of
time at our table during the dance. He would sit there
talking to us and, as subtly as possible, crane his neck
as he looked around to choose his next partner. When
he saw someone who attracted him, he would go over
and ask her to dance.

When the midnight buffet supper was served, the
Prince looked up from our table and said, "Your parents are up there. On that balcony." The White House
balcony was dark, but he had spotted them sitting on
porch chairs watching us. They had given a dinner
party for a small group of friends including Washington's "Princess" Alice, the daughter of Theodore Roosevelt. After dinner, my parents and their guests had
come out on the balcony to watch us dancing in the
tent of lights.

It seems to be impossible to spend time with a
public figure, a man who can be expected to be increasingly prominent as the decades pass, without remembering even the smallest details of his appearance.
I noted that Prince Charles wore a signet ring on his
fourth finger. His dancing shoes were elegant blue

velvet slippers embossed with the golden feathers of his crest as Prince of Wales. He was always well groomed, as befits someone who travels with a valet. He is of medium build, has rather long arms and a soft, melodious voice. And he has very pink cheeks, his most striking physical characteristic. At our first handshake, I glanced at him several times in quick succession, I was so struck by the inverted triangles of vivid pink on each cheekbone, which were of a velvety texture one might expect on the cheeks of a three-year-old who has been playing outdoors in the cold. It looked as if the color had been painted on with a fine-point brush, but it was completely natural.

I was not the only royalty watcher. Most of our guests studied him more or less openly and I admired the Prince's serene obliviousness of their scrutiny. I remembered reading about how, as a fourteen-year-old, Charles and several of his classmates from Gordonstoun, the Scottish boarding school he attended, had stopped at a small restaurant while they were on a school boat trip. "A lot of people were looking in the windows," young Charles said later, "and I thought 'I can't stand this any more' and went off." As it turned out the nearest place of escape from the noses pressed against the restaurant windows was the adjoining bar —where the Prince ordered a cherry brandy and thereby made headlines around the world. PRINCE CHARLES, A MINOR, ORDERS BRANDY IN BAR.

There had been scores of other excruciating journalistic invasions into his life as an adolescent. It must have been agony for a shy boy to have his academic progress publicized and even endure having his underpants publicly displayed. The latter happened in Australia when he spent six months of his junior year in high school at Timbertop School in the foothills of the Victorian Alps. His laundry was sent out with the rest of the school's—until one day his underpants were put on display in the laundry window. From then on, his weekly washing was done in the seclusion of the school lavatories.

Incidents like these helped to forge the steely self-confidence with which the Prince of Wales faces the world. I only once saw him even slightly disconcerted during his Washington visit. The Royal Family takes it for granted that crowds will gather to watch them launch a ship, plant a tree, or visit an infirmary. But the day of Prince Charles' well-publicized excursion to watch the lackluster Washington Senators play baseball at the Robert F. Kennedy Memorial Stadium, there were only 7,500 fans in the stadium, which can seat 45,000. At the first sight of those sun-scorched rows and rows of empty seats, Charles paled, then he flushed. But as I watched, I saw his attitude change rapidly from shock and disappointment to acceptance. And finally dismissal. He simply focused on other things. I very much doubt that he indulged in any late-night brooding.

It was only on the morning of Charles and Anne's last day in Washington that the source of many of the tensions I had felt during the visit became clear to me, and I began to appreciate the enormous achievement represented by the Prince of Wales' unfailing equanimity, his determined attempts to say a few words to as many people as he could, and his gift for putting people at ease. I also began to understand what lay behind so much of Princess Anne's discomfiture and aloofness during her stay—and to feel a very real sympathy for her.

Tricia and I had been waiting near the Queen's Bedroom for Princess Anne to join us for a tour of Georgetown. Her lady-in-waiting and friend, Lady Mary Dawnay, alerted us that the Princess was almost ready. Then we heard Anne close the door of her bedroom. We stood up and watched her come down the hall, an erect girl in a very short, sleeveless dress and sturdy walking shoes.

Lady Mary, who was at least ten years older than

Anne, dropped her knee almost to the floor in a deep, reverent curtsy. In that moment, I realized what it meant to be of royal birth. The Prince and Princess are ever conscious that they are royalty—and they expect obeisance, a constant deference. For three days, I had tried to relate to Charles and Anne as young visitors to our country, as two individuals close to my own age who had experienced some of the same privileges and penalties that come with being a public person. I had closed my eyes to the barrier imposed by royal birth, the barrier that is always maintained between the Royal Family and the rest of the world, scrupulously maintained even with those persons whom they know intimately. In America, Princess Anne must have suffered an abrupt culture shock, thrown into an environment where a careful distance between herself and others was not maintained, where there were few signs of reverence for her position in life.

Prince Charles once said, "I think one can be normal if one starts being an international person right from the word go. There is only a problem when you are thrown into it." After watching Charles and Anne together for three days, it was apparent, however, that the Prince has an idealized view of what being royal means. He assumes that royalty is immune from flattery and not affected by the extraordinary social insulation that is the result of—among other things—traveling with a staff hierarchy, which includes, for example, a lady-in-waiting who, in turn, is attended by a woman with the title "maid to the lady-in-waiting." Charles himself has come to grips with his position in life and has faced it with a good deal of courage and grace. It is a considerable personal achievement. But other royal personages unable to conquer shyness, or perhaps ill at ease or demanding, find it difficult to adjust to the world outside the family circle.

Charles speaks almost mystically about the role of

the monarchy. During the cruise on the Potomac, he told us that people have a strong desire for stability and that the monarchy supplies them with an anchor. When one guest suggested that it also filled a "fairy-tale need," Charles did not deny it. At the time he visited Washington, he seemed to believe that political heads of state appealed only to those who had voted for them. He had his belief slightly shaken the Friday morning of his visit when my father dropped in to say hello to the members of the band as they rehearsed for the dance that night. Charles was fascinated by the band leader's reaction and told me how the musician had described the encounter to him. "The President walked out," the band leader had said, "and goddamn—if he didn't shake my hand!" The Prince seemed astounded that members of a rock group could relate to a "conservative."

This did not, of course, shake his conviction that monarchy was a better form of government. Ours, he felt, was a less civilized system. He spoke of the common procedure of asking the President his views on every topic imaginable and the ensuing inevitable criticism of those views. "We aren't subject to that," Charles explained to the group that had gathered around him on the yacht. "Our views don't make a difference to people's everyday lives."

Yet, from reading the newspapers, it is clear that Charles' views on a wide range of subjects are being sought these days. And as for criticism, it has to be a matter of personal opinion which is the more demanding—a cruel political cartoon of the President or a newspaper photograph of Princess Anne on the back of a Land Rover at a review of troops with her skirt blown up around her waist and her underwear exposed.

Charles gave me the feeling that he had given more thought to his future marriage than to his future as King Charles or the relevancy of the monarchy in the space age. The night of the ball, the Prince talked briefly about what he wants in a wife. His desire that she come from a family background that "understands" the requirements of royalty narrowly limits his choices. Since that summer evening of the ball, the prospect of marriage has become somewhat of an obsession for the public and thus for Charles. He has no recent examples to follow: A Prince of Wales has not been married since 1863, when Queen Victoria's son Edward married Princess Alexandra of Denmark, the prettiest of the eligible princesses of the era. He does, however, have some clearcut guidelines. The Act of Succession prohibits him from marrying a Roman Catholic, and, as "Defender of the Faith," he would be in an uncomfortable position if he desired to marry a divorced woman.

He seems to have made his own rules. The head must rule the heart, he has said. Falling in love is not enough. His wife must also be his best friend. And his marriage will have to last forever. "Matrimony," he has stated, "is perhaps the biggest step one can take in life. A lot revolves around that decision . . . success or failure."

Success or failure, because the Prince's circle of friends will never be a large one. His wife's companionship will have to fulfill many needs. Charles' satisfaction and happiness in life will come more from the personal life that he and his wife will create within the confines of the royal residences than from the glittering pageantry and increasingly empty responsibilities of kingship.

Success or failure, because there is no room for error. No way out through divorce. His marriage will be subject to the same close scrutiny as everything else in his life. It will be watched closely for cracks and flaws. And it must survive the unusual strain of constant surveillance by an entourage of live-in servants, secretaries, equerries and ladies-in-waiting.

Success or failure, because Charles has the added pressure of being expected to produce a child to inherit his throne. And fatherhood is a role that seems to make the Prince uncomfortable. He has said that raising children is an "appalling" responsibility, a demanding job that must be undertaken jointly by mother and father, because "that is what marriage is all about. Creating a home."

Charles places so much importance on the family that he finds it difficult to understand women who believe they have missed opportunities to fulfill their potential because they have stayed at home and raised a family. He finds the stridency of the women's rights movement "uncivilized." And he has little sympathy for or comprehension of the frustrations and inequities that generated the movement. "There are quite a lot of things women don't want to do or can't do," he explains, "which men can do because we happen to be constructed differently in a physical sense."

The Prince of Wales laments that "men today do not often think of women as somewhat fragile characters who need caring for." Charles' view that the women's liberation movement tends to make men "less gallant" is appropriate for his future role as king-in-shining-armor, a king who will need a docile, supportive queen at his side. He is very much the product of upper-class English society—all-male boarding schools, a predominantly masculine university environment (women represent only fourteen percent of the enrollment at Cambridge), exclusive men's clubs and the military. To a great extent he has spent his life in a masculine world.

He has never known an existence without the constant shadow of a male detective, and at most times, the presence of an equerry as well. In fact, Charles says, "I was brought up mostly with older people." It is a strange statement on the face of it for a boy who was sent away to boarding school when he was only eight years old, but the explanation lies in the long school holidays in the royal household with the more than one hundred members of the Queen's court. His motto as Prince of Wales is *Ich dien* (I serve), but he is surrounded by people who serve him. His great-uncle, the Duke of Windsor, once tried to explain what an equerry was to Will Rogers, only to have Rogers respond, "I guess we have the same animal out in Oklahoma, only we call 'em hired hands." Charles will always have his staff, his equerries and his private secretaries to help him deal with people and circumstances in the outside world.

Because of the detectives, he has never experienced a "normal" degree of freedom, although he cannot be blind to the easier relationships that develop between his friends and the young women they date compared to his own encounters with dancing partners or weekend guests. Being forever protected by a bodyguard means there are very few spontaneous moments in his life. He cannot run out to buy a new record. Or take a walk late at night to clear his head. First of all, he must notify the detective, then allow him time to get his coat, keys, order a car or whatever. There must be occasions when the Prince questions whether the record or the walk is worth the effort.

I wonder if Charles, even though he has had Scotland Yard protection since the day he was born, is able to take for granted the constant presence of another person who—though it is an expected part of his job—may often have to wait for him hours on end in a drafty corridor or a cold car in winter or have to be away from his family on holidays. A president's child is not required to adjust completely to Secret Service surveillance because it is a temporary condition and ends once the term of office is over, so I cannot compare my feelings with those of Prince Charles, but I found that when my father was President I was never free from the realization that my every action involved another person.

The Prince has been aware that he is "different" from the time he was a toddler, but his school years heightened his sense of being apart more than any experience in his life. Charles had to resolve the schizophrenic tension of being a "normal," regular member of his school and then very much a prince on public occasions and within the palace walls. He had memories and experiences which his classmates could not relate to easily. One's early memory at age three of not being able to sleep at night because of the throngs of people who cheered Her Majesty Queen Elizabeth II on her coronation day is not the kind of experience one shares casually with friends.

It was difficult, he said, to make friends at school because the other boys were accused of "sucking up" to him. It is ironic that a prince, the symbol of privilege, must deal with the prejudice of those who make him feel that "I have to show people that I am a reasonable human being." It was the Prince who almost always had to make the effort to make a new friend. Charles has his own definition of true friends. "They are the ones," he says, "who never say anything to anybody about me, although they are always being asked about me and what I'm doing."

It is not surprising that at Cambridge University, Charles' major field of study was history. "I believe strongly one can learn a great deal from history," he said. "It enables us to interpret the present and the future." This may seem a belaboring of the obvious, but for Charles, history was a key to understanding his role and coping with the problems of being a public person for all of his life. "I still think there is an awful lot of rot which is written about people who existed two or three hundred years ago. But they were human beings," he said, "and they had feelings and sensitivities." It is not hard to hear an echo of his adolescent years when his own feelings and sensitivities were most acute and when the news stories and pronouncements about his appearance or his potential must have been embarrassing and often hurtful.

Even in the palace-authorized biography by the man who holds the title of Arundel Herald Extraor-

Talking with Mrs. Meir in her retirement office in Ramat Aviv, one day after the third anniversary of the Yom-Kippur War, the war which caused Golda to say "I will never again be the same person . . ." I.P.P.A. LTD.

Clara Stern's favorite photograph of her famous sister. REGINALD DAVIS

Israel's first woman Prime Minister is greeted by my father at the North Portico of the White House in 1973. "She never wanted to be treated like a woman, but like a leader," he told me.

Ruth and Billy Graham in Hong Kong in 1975, the closest point Ruth has been to mainland China since she left the land of her birth in 1937 to attend Wheaton College in Illinois. At Wheaton she met a fellow student named Billy Graham.

Ruth reading in the window seat of the big log cabin house in Montreat, North Carolina, she and Billy built in 1956. From the window Ruth has a view of the Blue Ridge.
RUSS BUSBY

Motorcycling is one of Ruth Graham's favorite pastimes. Here she gets a lesson from her son Franklin's friend and his little boy.

The Grahams outside their house in Montreat. "Bill," Ruth said, "is telling me for the tenth time that month that my hair would look a whole lot prettier in the sunshine if it were brown instead of gray."

Anne Morrow Lindbergh at work in her writing studio, an old toolshed the Lindberghs found on Route 1 not far from their home in Darien, Connecticut. RICHARD BROWN

Anne with her youngest child, Reeve, and her granddaughter. Reeve told me, "We all worry about her constantly but she is, in fact, invincible." RICHARD BROWN

*Ike and Mamie in the yard of their son's home on their golden
wedding anniversary, July 1, 1966.* BRADFORD BACHRACH

Mamie, my mother and I on the inaugural platform shortly before my father took the oath of office for his second term. Behind us, left to right, Attorney General Richard Kleindienst, Secretary of the Treasury George Shultz and Secretary of State William Rogers.
WHITE HOUSE PHOTO

My family in front of the White House on Inauguration Day, January 20, 1973. Since David was on Naval duty in the Mediterranean, Mamie told everyone, "I'm playing David."
WHITE HOUSE PHOTO

Mamie and I celebrating her birthday, November 14, 1974, at a small inn in Gettysburg. The photograph was taken by one of her Secret Service agents.

A proud moment: Mamie christens the 95,000-ton aircraft carrier named in honor of her husband. UPI

The highlight of the three-day visit to Washington of 20-year-old Prince Charles and his 19-year-old sister Anne was the ball at the White House for 600 young people. WHITE HOUSE PHOTO

We danced on a platform erected on the South Lawn of the White House under a "tent" of thousands of tiny electric lights, and a full July moon. WHITE HOUSE PHOTO

In sweltering 90-degree weather we tried to explain baseball to Prince Charles and Princess Anne.

*A less than gregarious moment on board the Presidential yacht
Sequoia as we journeyed down the Potomac River to Mount
Vernon for a tour of George Washington's estate. David and I are
at the left; the Princess is second from right.*

At two minutes to midnight on New Year's Eve 1975 we met Chairman Mao at his home deep within the Forbidden City. His niece Wang Hai-jung watches as David grasps the Chairman's hand.

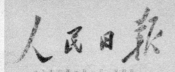
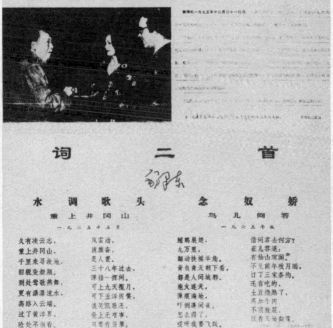

The People's Daily *on New Year's Day 1976. Below the photograph of the Chairman greeting us are two poems by Mao in which he exhorts his people to continue the revolution and resist Soviet revisionism.*

Dozens of smiling Chinese students were studying posters denouncing the Minister of Education when we visited Tsinghua University in Peking.

dinary, the court biographer Dermot Morrah, the Prince of Wales was described as 'intellectually rather young for his years." There were similar comments from teachers and friends that he was a "late bloomer," a safe term to use because the same had been said of the young Winston Churchill. It was as if they found it necessary to find excuses for the young Prince with average grades and a pronounced shyness. It can be considered a personal triumph that Charles was finally able to acknowledge, "I may have been slightly late in developing"—and put it all behind him.

Possibly the most revealing public comment Charles has ever made about himself—for anyone who admits loneliness is vulnerable—is "The older I get, the more alone I become." He spoke these words with matter-of-fact acceptance. This is, this will be his life. A life apart. A life of loneliness. And the cruelest form of loneliness may be to feel lonely in a crowd.

I had a small glimpse of how that loneliness pervades almost every facet of his life when Charles visited us in Washington. He is lonely because so rarely can he be honest and candid with others. In the course of three days our conversations were lively and wide-ranging, but superficial. I learned that he played the cello and the trumpet, that he likes to act in private theatricals, that he does watercolors. I learned that he is interested in preserving the natural resources of this planet. But I learned very little about his concerns or personal struggles as an individual or his views on the issues facing his country.

There were many questions that I wanted to ask him. Trivial ones, but ones that might reveal the person. When he spoke of his requirements for a future consort I wanted to ask him more about a statement I had read, in which he was quoted as saying that he would not marry before age thirty. David and I had been married for almost a year. I wondered what he thought about early marriages. I doubted that many of his young friends were married, since Englishmen of the upper classes marry quite late.

I had a dozen questions of this sort, but they went unasked, partly because I knew how difficult it was to be constantly subjected to personal questions, and partly because they seemed inappropriate. I was equally cautious when it came to political issues. Only six weeks earlier, Washington had been the scene of demonstrations against the war by 100,000 people, most of them our age. And there was the surprise victory in England of Edward Heath and the Conservative Party. All these issues existed, but like submerged icebergs, they were invisible and unmentionable in the company of the Prince, because Charles is at liberty to express opinions on a very limited number of topics not only in public but also in private gatherings as well. It is not just a matter of offending some segment of public opinion. He cannot appear to influence issues. Even with friends, he must think before he speaks, weigh whether or not something he says will be leaked.

The Prince of Wales spent an hour and fifteen minutes alone in the Oval Office with my father on the last afternoon of his visit. My father purposely had no aides present, so that the substance of their conversation would remain confidential. When I asked my father six years later about their conversation he told me that he had been impressed by Charles' ". . . extraordinary interest in and understanding of the entire world scene. Not just the problems of his own country. I found that he cared, he cared a great deal," my father said, "about building a world of peace and about the responsibilities that all nations have to try to achieve that goal." He also said that the Prince had been most interested in the problems of the emerging nations, the new African countries.

My father had been surprised by Charles. He found him assured, yet totally lacking in arrogance or self-importance. But he did not give the impression that he was an "ordinary" man. He was very conscious of

110

the duties his birth had placed upon him. My father had not expected him to be so articulate and informed. He was a different person than he had been led to expect from press reports and briefing papers.

I was surprised, because I had spent the better part of three days with Charles and while he was certainly articulate, I had not been aware of great intelligence or an informed grasp of events. But it was different with my father. My father was a head of state. The Prince of Wales could talk to him substantively. The world at large, however, will never witness the Prince's interaction with another world leader nor learn the details of his dealings with his Prime Ministers when he does ascend the throne. Never perceive more than a hint of the depth of the man. Because Charles is almost literally muzzled by the nonpartisan nature of the monarchy.

The inevitable result is that there is little incentive for him to think deeply about political or social issues, for if one thinks deeply, one begins to care about the actions that are taken. Or not taken. He cannot support further nationalization of industry, neither can he oppose it. It is hardly surprising then that when Charles does express an opinion, he tends to sound shallow. He has been forced to become a master of the innocuous generality.

One subject Charles is free to comment on is his ancestry. Of all his ancestors, Charles has stated that King George III is the monarch he most admires. He believes that the King "had a very raw deal through the history books," and his litany of George's virtues—sense of humor, marvelously eccentric, great human being, and English country gentleman, well-liked, comfortable—is a jarring contrast to the more familiar textbook characterization of this king whose reign was marked by the loss of the American colonies and who was considered by many of his contemporaries to be retarded as a child, neurotic, and ultimately insane as an adult.

Charles' fascination with and sympathy for George III is quite understandable though in light of the theory that the King suffered from porphyria, an hereditary metabolic disease. Two British physicians published a study in 1969 in which they concluded that this disorder in the body chemistry caused George III to experience delusion, hallucination and psychoses. The British doctors believe that porphyria has afflicted four centuries of royalty, beginning with Mary, Queen of Scots.

When Prince Charles visited us in Washington a year after the report was issued, he seemed fascinated by this explanation for George III's depression. The Prince discussed the disease at dinner with my family the evening of his return to England. The subject of the King's depression and madness seemed to spring from nowhere. We were gathered close around the small, dark mahogany table in the family dining room on the second floor of the White House. The only light was the soft glow of candles. The room was pleasantly cool and a fire in the fireplace added to the feeling of intimacy and relaxation. My father had put on a tape of classical music and the tension and fatigue of the visit dropped away as if by magic. There were no more people to meet, no more galleries to tour, no more monuments to admire. That scorchingly hot afternoon at the ball park seemed far away. Within hours, Charles and Anne would be home in their own rooms in their own beds.

Charles seemed to particularly enjoy my mother. He was sitting on her right and I was facing him across the table. They were talking absorbedly when I overheard the word "porphyria," and I listened as he told her about the study and the subsequent new perspective on George III's supposed madness. Ironically, we were literally surrounded by scenes on every inch of the papered walls of British soldiers battling the American revolutionists during George III's reign.

For the first time Charles was speaking to us with

feeling. He was acutely aware that the hereditary disease could manifest itself in the present generation —in his sister, his brothers, in himself. The symptoms, including the periods of derangement, do not appear until the victim is adult, and there is no known way as yet of preventing or curing porphyria. As I listened and watched him, so earnest and yet so debonair, I realized that not only his entire life but also his lineage is scrutinized. There are so many eager to compare him to past monarchs and to predict what he is capable of, and what he will become.

From all that the "Charles watchers" in Britain and the world can discern, the Prince is an exceptionally balanced and confident individual. He projects a cool image. His careful, measured approach to life is part of his heritage from his mother, a woman whose face registers few emotions in all the millions of photographs that have been taken of her. His smooth, confident manner is the mark of an individual who has defined the outer reaches of his role as heir apparent with great precision. "The one thing I cannot afford to do is get left miles behind," he explains. "Likewise you don't want to be too far ahead. You want to be just a little bit behind, but ready to adapt gently and slowly—and in some cases take the initiative."

The job for which he has spent his life preparing may not be his for decades to come. His ability and willingness to adapt may help him in the years ahead. And when he does ascend the throne, his adaptability will enable him to accept a role that has almost no power.

The totality of this lack of power has its ludicrous aspects. If Parliament were to pass a bill for the monarch's execution, the monarch would be forced to sign it—or abdicate. The Prince of Wales has lightheartedly commented, "In company with convicts, lunatics and peers of the realm, I am ineligible to vote." But at the same time he absolutely disagrees with those who say the throne is less powerful today than under Queen Victoria. He defines the monarch's power as an "influence which is unseen, often unfelt by the general public." His definition may remind some of the emperor's new clothes, but Charles has to believe in this power. Without it, his life would be frighteningly empty and purposeless.

He also seems to derive a sense of power from the mystical solemnity with which he invests the monarchy. In his memoirs, the Duke of Windsor vividly portrayed the reverence which is accorded the monarch in his description of the death of his father. Queen Mary was holding her husband's hand. As King George V drew his last breath, she gently withdrew her hand and took the hand of Edward, her eldest son, and kissed it. Prince Charles is heir to that kind of reverence. Much of his power will come from his ability to preserve this spiritual aura.

Prince Charles believes that influence, which is royalty's power, is "in direct ratio to the respect people have for you." Yet how, within the restraints of his princeship, can Charles earn the respect of his subjects? When he took his seat in the House of Lord's in 1970, the *London Times* called it "a link to history without any pretense of political significance."

He knows that Britons no longer take the monarchy for granted. Some feel that it is an anachronism, affectionately tolerated at the moment, but nevertheless out of place in today's world. And many of her financially beleaguered subjects view the Queen more as head of a privileged establishment than as head of the country, a view supported by the fact that the palace entourage is drawn exclusively from the upper classes. Charles is eager to counter the criticism. "One has to be far more professional at it [the monarchy], I think, than you ever used to be," he states. For example, he has established a "Prince's Trust," with a committee dispensing the funds, designed to help young people find "adventure, excitement, and satisfaction" by undertaking their own self-help projects. The trust has provided immigrant youth with funds to pay for driving lessons; another group was given enough money to clear an abandoned lot and buy football equipment. Also, by granting occasional magazine, newspaper and television interviews, he is breaking new ground for the Royal Family.

As heir apparent, he has felt the need to justify his existence, but once he ascends the throne, he firmly believes he will be transformed into "one of the strongest factors in the continuance of stable government." He is convinced that Great Britain will never crumble as a nation unless she loses sight of her values and principles and, in his view, the monarchy is the safeguard against such a loss.

Charles is very sure of those values. He does not mind being called square. "I may be square today," he has said, "but not in ten years' time. . . . As far as I'm concerned, I'm going to go on believing to a certain extent in certain things that I consider to be true and right, decent and honorable." This conviction may explain the Prince's serene public face.

But a great many young Britons find the "certain things" he believes in as relevant as the Queen Mother's baroquely flowered hats. When Charles was invested as Prince of Wales in 1969, a fellow student at Cambridge wrote him an open letter: "We should like to have a king who is not afraid to speak out against hypocrisy and inhumanity," he wrote. "No doubt they will want to put you in the British Navy. . . . They will give you a smart blue uniform and a stiff upper lip; we would rather give you a girl, a grin and a purpose in life."

It may be that the future king will yet find a way to personify purpose and service, to win the respect of the younger generation that has inherited the complicated and humbling problems of adjusting from a global power to an island nation dependent upon mutual ties of trade with other countries. Charles and his generation face a crisis of spirit, characterized by an apathy about work and a feeling of helplessness about the economic and social problems that have weakened Great Britain. If Charles could create a new spirit of hope and idealism, encourage an ethic of work and achievement, he might at the same time invest the monarchy with more meaning than it has today.

If the skeptical younger Britons could know the Prince of Wales, they would discover a rare conversationalist, a trivia expert, a good judge of human nature, and a man with a sense of humor that helps him withstand his often tedious ceremonial duties. He has described the image in his mind as he launches a ship—"The champagne bottle hits the bow, tiny cracks appear on the surface of the ship, and two tons precisely and beautifully fall apart."

They might also discover that they had something in common with this Prince who, because he has been "different" from birth, has tried to understand the minds and hearts of "normal" people, just as he tries to strip away false assumptions about himself and asks people to accept him for what he is.

When asked, "Wouldn't you like to be free?" his answer is: "Being free isn't doing what other people like you to do, it's doing what you like to do." In whatever he does, Charles tries to project the image of a young man doing his job. But one cannot resist asking if a young man of his potential should be sentenced to a lifetime of more show than substance.

The Prince is accorded the sustained press, public interest and even homage that is reserved for heroes. It is the kind of attention that touches the celebrities of our television age only fleetingly. Yet the only heroic thing Charles has ever done was to be born a prince: an instant personage. His mother, then heiress presumptive to the throne, gave birth at 9:14 P.M. Three hours later, at a quarter past midnight, the enthusiasm of the celebrating crowds who had gathered in front of Buckingham Palace had to be subdued by police loudspeakers announcing: "The Palace has requested a little quiet, if you please." Yet Elizabeth welcomed the cheers as a sign of tribute to the throne. She was a mother—and a princess. The human symbol—and the mystical. Accessibility—and remoteness.

In almost three days of shared experiences, I never really felt close to Prince Charles. The lack of rapport was not simply due to the famous English reserve. There was something more. He held himself apart. It was the royal barrier. Charles was unspoiled, good-humored, concerned—and yet royal and aloof.

As we shook hands in farewell, he said cordially, "You must come over and visit us soon." But I knew I probably never would have contact with him again except through the lens of a camera or from the viewpoint of a reporter. The media will inform me if he gets a speeding ticket, has a son, or loses his hair.

With the rest of the world, I will watch Charles as he strikes the delicate balance between relating to others as a human being and accepting the fact of his royal birth, which destines him one day to be anointed with holy oil and hailed by the peers of the realm with the cry, "God Save the King! God Save the King! God Save the King!"

*Anne
Morrow
Lindbergh*

———— ————

"Life is a gift, given in trust—like
a child."

ANNE LINDBERGH loved to fly. It put a "glaze over life," she wrote. "There is no crack in the surface." Life was "somehow arrested and frozen into form." Ironically, it must often seem to Anne Lindbergh as if she herself had truly been "arrested and frozen into form," one March night many years ago, frozen into an unwanted and almost inescapable image. The image of a bereaved mother. The woman whose perceptive *Gift from the Sea* has solaced and encouraged generations of other women, whose diaries reveal a keen intellect, an unflinching candor and a tempestuously emotional soul, is still less real to many people than the decades-old image of a bereaved mother.

A year after the kidnapping and murder of her eighteen-month-old son, Charles Augustus Lindbergh, Jr., Anne Lindbergh wrote in her diary, "I think about it all the time—it never stops—I never meet it. It happens every night—every night of my life." She did learn how to meet it, but she has called that facing of truth the most difficult task of her life. The last sentence in her diary entry for that day in 1933, "I will never be through with it," was to be prophetic.

I visited Mrs. Lindbergh at her home in Darien, Connecticut, in the spring and fall of 1976, more than forty-three years after she wrote those words. As we sat in her living room during my second visit, drinking tea and looking out over the peaceful waters of Scott's Cove, I learned how truly she had foreseen the future. We were talking casually about the volume of mail she receives and she had told me how much she dislikes resorting to form letters, yet the hours that she spends on her correspondence eats into the time she wants to devote to her writing. I suggested that she try to ignore as much of the mail as possible for several days at a stretch and then answer it in one concentrated effort.

"But there are always letters I can't ignore," she said, and went over to her desk. She came back with a telegram, a request for her comment on a just-published book which argued that Bruno Richard Hauptmann, the man convicted of the kidnapping and murder of her baby, was innocent. Mrs. Lindbergh read the telegram to me quickly and then put it down on her lap and folded her hands over it. Her eyes were wide, distressed. I did not know what to say. She spoke first, "It just never ends."

She will never escape completely that image of the bereaved mother, but she has been able to overcome it to a great degree because of her intense desire to communicate with others. Communicating has not come easily to Anne Lindbergh. One of her greatest obstacles, she said, is that she has felt "separated" from life. As we talked she returned to the word "separated" again and again.

"I had to break through quite a lot to find myself. It's a perpetual process. I'm still learning."

"What is the barrier? What is it that you find so separating?" I asked.

Mrs. Lindbergh thought for perhaps half a minute before she could find the precise words. Then she answered, "It was a very polite and gentle world I lived in."

Her father, Dwight L. Morrow, was a senior partner of J. P. Morgan, the international bankers. Anne described a life to me that revolved around family. Her brother and two sisters were her playmates and together they invented many of their own games. They wrote poetry and short stories and shared them with one another. They attended private schools. Like many wealthy New York families, the Morrows traveled abroad frequently.

When her father became Ambassador to Mexico in 1927, "a whole new life" opened up for Anne Morrow, the life of diplomacy. But she found when she joined her family in Mexico City during her vacations from Smith College that "even official life is separating." The large garden parties, the teas, luncheons and dinners with a limited group of people and the often superficial conversation seemed to isolate her family and acquaintances from the world.

"Then I married Charles," Anne continued. "This seemed to be real life."

But she had married a hero.

Charles Lindbergh came from a world far removed from that of Anne Morrow. He was a Minnesota farm boy, more interested in cultivating the land and in all things mechanical—especially automobiles and airplanes—than he was in literature or art. His mother, a high-school chemistry teacher, encouraged his technical interests, and his father, who had served in Congress as a Progressive Republican from 1906 to 1917, showed Charles the excitement and adventure of the outdoors, but taught him very little about politics or world affairs. Unlike Anne, who was an honors graduate of Smith, Charles left the University of Wisconsin in 1922 after three semesters to become a barnstorming pilot. In 1926, he was flying mail between St. Louis and Chicago in his own plane. And in 1927, this unknown airmail pilot took off from Roosevelt Field on Long Island on his way to Paris and glory.

Lindbergh's nonstop flight across the Atlantic was already a legend when Anne met him a year later when he stayed with the Morrows at the American Embassy during his goodwill visit to Mexico. From the moment the *Spirit of St. Louis* had landed at Le Bourget in Paris, Charles was the golden young man of America and Europe. He was brave—he had flown alone. He was modest and upright—a refreshing contrast to the cheap commercialism and spiritual emptiness of the Roaring Twenties. The conservative *New York Times* devoted its first five pages to his flight. One hundred thousand school children sang "Hail the Conquering Hero Comes" to welcome him to New York, while a crowd of four and a half million people cheered and pelted him with confetti.

When Anne Morrow married Charles in May of 1929, he was a hero to her as well. What appealed most to Anne as she fell in love with her hero was his "clarity . . . never a false note." But the world would never know the Charles Lindbergh she loved, never see him with clarity. He, too, was trapped in an image —first that of the All-American hero, and later in another image, almost the reverse side of the coin, that of the racist and the man who was "wrong" about World War II.

Marriage did not prove to be the open door into "real life" that Anne had expected. "Fame separates you from life," she told me that afternoon in Darien. When she said this I immediately thought of her description in her book *Hour of Gold, Hour of Lead* of what had happened when she married her hero and became part of the legend herself. "Fame is a kind of death," she had written, "it arrests life around you." I remembered those words because I had agreed with them. It is more difficult for the person in the public eye to communicate with others. You become cautious and circumspect. It dampens your spirit. It is easy to lose one's perspective.

Anne Lindbergh found fame a high price to pay for love and adventure. From the very beginning she disliked being recognized. Shortly after the wedding, she wrote her mother, "I have no patience, no understanding, no sympathy with the people who stare and follow and giggle at us." Neither Anne nor her husband ever learned to accept the public's interest in them.

I had often wondered if Anne Lindbergh had realized how changed her life would be when she married Charles Lindbergh, and if part of Charles' attraction for her was that he was a hero. The night before my graduation from The Chapin School in New York, there was a party for seniors. As part of the school tradition, each of us filled out a questionnaire about our plans and dreams for the future. What we wanted to do with our lives. Where we would like to live. Did we want to have children? And how many? When one senior protested, saying it was "silly," the headmistress smiled and said, "One day you will be very interested." She went on to tell us that Anne Lindbergh, a member of the class of 1924, had written in response to the question about the kind of man she wanted to marry, "I want to marry a hero."

I remembered this story the first time I saw Mrs. Lindbergh. It was during my senior year at Smith College. She had made a rare visit to her alma mater to speak on the environment. Standing alone on the huge stage facing the two thousand students who had come to hear her, she looked small and lost. It was easy to think of her as the helpless victim of an infamous crime, but once she began to speak, she was forceful and I was captured by her words.

Later that afternoon, David and I had tea with her at the home of the president of the college. Her sister and brother-in-law, Constance and Aubrey Morgan, President and Mrs. Mendenhall, and David and I were waiting around the fireplace in the living room when Anne slipped into the room like a shy schoolgirl. She had changed into a skirt and sweater. Her body was slight, almost fragile. And the slight pull of her lips to one side when she smiled gave her a vulnerable, sweet expression.

We talked for more than an hour, mostly about world population problems. As a woman who had given birth to six children, she was quick to acknowledge a certain irony in her present concern about overpopulation. It would have been easy to underestimate the delicate woman whose head barely reached the top of her wing chair, to overlook the strength beneath her quiet until she spoke. She was self-effacing and gentle, but she gave the impression that she truly wanted to exchange ideas. She listened to others, her face intent as she absorbed their words, and she made her own points without trying to impress or compete, skillfully interjecting fresh ideas, then generously allowing others to expand on them. When we said good-bye, she had dispelled all images. She was not the "wife of an American hero," not a "tragic figure," not a "famous author." She was her own woman, full of ideas and eager to share them with the world, receptive to the thoughts of others.

We met again six years later in Darien. Her simple five-room house reflects the philosophy of Charles Lindbergh's later years, a philosophy Anne shared, of preserving natural beauty and of simple living. There are no traces of her husband now, no photographs or memorabilia of the young flyer. The only photograph, a beautiful scene of a forest at dusk shrouded in mist, was taken by their son-in-law. There is little else in the living room to distract from the beauty of Scott's Cove outside the large picture windows. This isolated stretch of water that opens into Long Island Sound is a sanctuary for geese and swans and other wildlife. It has been a sanctuary for the Lindberghs too. "My husband found it so very, very painful to be stared at, to be recognized," she said. Here on Scott's Cove, they were freer than they had ever been from this recognition.

They built this little house in 1963, the year their daughter Reeve, their youngest child, entered college. In the winter, when the trees are bare, Anne can see their old home only a few hundred yards away at the edge of the cove, a big house with plenty of room for five children and their friends. This house is different—small, tidy, functional. The way Anne lines up her shoes on the bathroom floor is a key to the philosophy of the house—the well-worn tennis shoes, the walking shoes, even her slippers are lined up in a corner, edge touching edge, not a precious inch of space wasted.

The living room serves as study and dining room as well. Anne often eats on a tray in front of the fire or beside the corner window overlooking the cove. Old cardboard cartons and typing-paper boxes, full of letters and other papers, are lined up on her desk, the desk that belonged to her father, and cover the top of the file cabinet beside it.

It was at that desk that Charles Lindbergh helped Anne with the first two volumes of her letters and diaries. He helped put the letters into categories. He read galleys. And he gave her courage—especially when she was working on the difficult second volume that dealt with the kidnapping and death of their son. Some of the Lindbergh children have never been able to force themselves to read that second volume.

In their last years together, when they lived in this small house, they seemed to regain some of the camaraderie of the 1930s when Charles was pilot and Anne his radio operator and navigator and they charted new air routes around the world. But now Anne Lindbergh is alone in the house. Alone she must live with her memories and sort out the images that fame created of her and her husband.

Criticisms of her husband are no more easy to bear now than when he was alive. She cannot bring herself to read the latest biography which repeats the old charges of anti-Semitism and of his distrust of democracy. Her reluctance has nothing to do with cowardice or an avoidance of reality, it is rather that she cannot face what she believes to be a view so distorted that it is unreal. More than that, she cannot skim such a book that puts her own stubborn loyalties into question, because Anne Lindbergh does not approach anything casually. Even when she expresses an idea in an informal conversation, she does so thoughtfully, conscious of every word and its meaning. There were times when answering one of my questions, she still seemed to be thinking about the previous one, her dark blue eyes far away, her body slightly hunched.

We talked about her husband, what he was really like. "He was someone utterly opposed to me," she had confided in her diary when she first met him.

"We were totally different," she told me. "He felt living was more important than writing," but she smiled ruefully and added, "He expressed himself very well when he wrote. Even his crash landing reports when he was an airmail pilot were good."

At first, Anne immersed herself in the world of this man who was so different, the world that seemed to be real life. "I lived adventure," she told me, "but I am not sure I would do all that traveling again." Her comment surprised me, because I had been wedded to the romantic idea of Charles and Anne Lindbergh flying off together, meeting the challenge of long, grueling hours in the air, flying over the Alps, landing their seaplane in the Yangtze River in China. Always together. But in the prefaces to her four volumes of diaries, Anne Lindbergh warns constantly—beware of images; don't freeze someone in your mind; allow people to grow and to change.

I suspect that Charles Lindbergh realized early in their marriage, possibly even before she did, that the "real world" for Anne was her writing. Under his tutelage she had become the first woman to earn a glider pilot's license and she had qualified as a radio operator, yet even as she entered his world, he was encouraging her to write. And his encouragement was not just verbal. He helped her, including drawing the maps, with her first two books, *North to the Orient* and *Listen, the Wind,* which described their round-the-world flights in 1931 and 1933.

Reading her diaries between 1929 and 1939, it becomes clear that she was torn during the first ten years of her marriage between wanting to be part of his world of action and wanting time alone to write. She was angry with herself in 1934 for her reluctance to go on a long trip. "I should be grateful to Charles," she wrote, "for pulling me out of my rut where I would always stay in my timidity if it were not for him." And four years later, as they were about to leave for the Soviet Union, she wrote, "I must go. I must be part of Charles' life."

But she needed freedom, too. Anne and Charles Lindbergh needed different kinds of freedom. Their youngest child, Reeve Lindbergh Brown, says that her father needed the outer freedom to "get up and get going," and her mother needed the inner freedom of time alone to think and write.

Charles Lindbergh's overwhelming energy was matched by his power of concentration. He would sit down and write for three hours after a seven-mile hike. He was an exuberant man, overpraising those he loved ("Your mother is the greatest author of the twentieth century"), and giving his wife and children the feeling that they could do anything. When he was with Anne and their children or with friends, he was frequently the most talkative of the group—in contrast to his taciturnity with the press and strangers.

"My mother was calm and calming," Reeve told me, "although she did not think of herself that way. When my father was away, Mother was not so much a disciplinarian as she was an example." And when Charles Lindbergh came home, he was such a strong and absorbing person that, according to Reeve, "He seemed to demand more oxygen than there was air. He would fill up the house, and they would co-exist."

They co-existed throughout their marriage, because they respected each other so much, despite different working styles, different needs and different ideas. Fame separated them from the rest of the world and they became each other's confidants and best friends. Having to be guarded with casual acquaintances because something might be leaked to the press was one root of their feeling of separateness, especially in the early years. At her husband's suggestion, Anne was even careful about what she said in letters to her family and friends. On her own initiative, she stopped keeping her diaries. But the kidnapping changed that. Three days before the baby's body was found in the woods a few miles from their home, Anne returned to her journal to preserve her sanity.

Public interest in the tragedy was intense. After the baby was stolen from its second-floor bedroom in the Lindbergh's home, the general manager of the United Press stated, "I can't think of any story that would compare with it unless America should enter a war." There was ten weeks of incessant publicity as Charles Lindbergh negotiated with people who claimed— falsely—to have clues. Two years later, there was another six weeks in the spotlight and the private horror of reliving the crime when Hauptmann was brought to trial.

From the time their second son, Jon, was born in August, 1932, five months after the murder of his brother, the Lindbergh family lived under the protection of armed guards whom they hired to shield them from the curious, from the press, and from lunatics. In her diary, Anne revealed just how separated from the world she felt in those years. When she was trying to find a nursery school for Jon, she had "a dread," she wrote, "of sending Jon out into that strange world C and I are in, where we are 'different.' "

Finally, three days before Christmas in 1935, the Lindberghs fled the country. In the secret of night, they boarded a passenger-freighter bound for England —and what they hoped would be a new life. Many Americans could not understand why they left. They had showered Charles Lindbergh with honors and acclaim. They had wept with him and for him. Now they resented losing their hero. But no one, not even Charles Lindbergh, until years later, knew the desperation that Anne expressed in her journal in the weeks before the abrupt decision to leave.

"I must control my mind—I must control my body —I must control my emotions—I must finish the book —I must put up an appearance at least of calm for C . . . but last night lying in bed, shrinking over into my corner, trying not to cry . . . not to wake C, trying not to toss or turn, trying to be like a stone . . . I felt I could understand insanity and physical violence. I could understand anything."

I asked her if she had any regrets about the three and a half years they lived abroad, in England and France. Despite the party atmosphere of our English tea, she left no room for cordiality or discussion in answering. "No, we had to go away. I couldn't have a baby. It was worth it for that."

After a year of relative quiet and peace, her third child, Land, was born in a London hospital in 1937. He was five years younger than his brother Jon.

The kidnapping brought Anne and Charles even closer together, because they lost so much faith in others. But their later grief separated them. They reacted differently to grief.

"Charles entered a totally different and, for him, private world," Anne told me. He studied the effects of high-altitude flying on man with Nobel-Prize winner Dr. Alexis Carrel. "My way out," she told me, was writing in her diaries and completing her first book, *North to the Orient*.

In a rare personal comment, Charles Lindbergh revealed his lifelong attitude toward written expression in his 1941 wartime journal: "I can seldom, if ever, put my deepest feelings into words." And yet the woman he married wrote about everything—even her grief. I shrink when I think of Anne Lindbergh's honesty in recording the daily horrors of the kidnapping and its aftermath. Writing it down made it real. It was no longer possible for her to believe "this isn't really happening to me." It was happening. And at the end of each day she relived it all in her diary. And she cried. But secretly, so that her husband and mother, who were captives of what she has described as the "stoic tradition of hiding grief," would not know.

As the years have passed, Anne Lindbergh has become convinced that expressing emotion is part of facing tragedy. She knows now that the healing would have come faster if she had communicated more of her grief to her husband.

"My parents and their generation," she told me, "were very moral and upright. Yet they were dishonest in being so stoical and not expressing emotion —whether it was about love or death." Not expressing emotion was denying life in a way. It meant that one took on what Anne Lindbergh calls "protective shells." But she rejected such shells. She wanted life. All of life, including the hurt.

Much of the hurt she would face in the years following the kidnapping stemmed from her husband's lingering bitterness toward the press because of their often ghoulish reporting of the crime, and from his obsession with what he regarded as the media's unwillingness to distinguish between his private and public life. "Charles simply could not understand anyone being interested in one's private life," she told me. "He just couldn't bear it," she added, her voice very soft—and sad. Charles Lindbergh came to loathe the intrusions of the press and he lost faith in their ability to report factually what he did and said.

When the American press reported erroneously in 1938 that the Lindberghs planned to rent a house in Berlin owned by an evicted Jew, Anne was terribly upset, but as she recorded in her diary, "C is marvelously untouched by all of it. Their scorn does not touch him any more than their praise once did."

In reality, however, the family, if not Charles, was touched. The press resented Lindbergh's disdain, and they resented even more the stigma of being the cause of his flight abroad. Lindbergh's public opposition to the United States' entry into World War II made him a legitimate subject for criticism for those who disagreed with his position. And because he would not explain what he meant by certain statements or employ the usual political tact in his isolationist speeches, his opponents' attack on him was tragically devastating.

"We are all still reeling from it, though in general the public has forgotten the whole business," says Reeve Lindbergh Brown, who was not even born until after World War II ended. Reeve's awakening came as a teenager. "When I learned that because of my father's war speeches some people saw him as a bigot, I was dumbfounded," she wrote me. "Reading things that were said about him during the war; parents of certain of my friends acting a little oddly toward me; a roommate of one boy I went out with telling my friend, 'Well, I don't mind meeting her, but you'll never get me to shake hands with her father'; and all the time, nothing corresponded to *my* view of my father, so that each experience of this kind was a crazy kind of nightmare."

Charles Lindbergh had experienced a similar nightmare, although on a more limited scale, when his father was hanged in effigy and denounced for his opposition to World War I. It was a strange repeat of history that saw Charles Lindbergh become the most prominent isolationist of his generation.

In 1936 during several trips to Germany arranged by Truman Smith, military attaché of the American Embassy in Berlin, so that Lindbergh could gather intelligence on German aircraft production for the United States, he concluded that America was the only country in the world that could compete with German air power. At the same time, he became convinced that American participation in a European war would be a disaster. Consequently, when the war started in Europe, Lindbergh, for the first time in his life, welcomed the spotlight that followed him because he wanted to use the publicity to warn against the coming danger.

He joined the America First Committee, the most powerful isolationist pressure group, in 1940. And he spoke over and over again at America First rallies warning that if America came to England's aid, the war would be prolonged and lead to a greater devastation of Europe, especially Europe's democracies—and perhaps lead to the loss of freedoms in the United States as well. One of his greatest fears was that America would become a regimented, militaristic society.

Anne Lindbergh aligned herself with the movement against American entry into the war with her book *The Wave of the Future,* published in 1940. It was an emotional appeal from an intellectual who was more of an artist than a politician, an appeal for this country to reform itself, to reaffirm the spirit of sacrifice and democracy. "If we had really lived up to what we believed democracy was, would there ever have been any Nazism?" she asked a few weeks after the book was published.

More than thirty years later, she told me, "I am not at all a political person." I understood that. A politically conscious person would not have written *The Wave of the Future.* At the time she had naively described herself as "an average citizen attempting to state the problem clearly, not to offer a solution." But she was not an average citizen. She was a famous—and vulnerable—personality. Today she acknowledges that those who called her a "confused pacifist" did so "with some justification. I learned slowly, more slowly than most people, that there were worse things than war."

Anne and Charles Lindbergh were caught in a political world where they did not belong. In Anne's world of writing and Charles' world of adventure and science, they fortified and encouraged each other, but in this world of politics, they seemed unable to help each other. Lindbergh allowed his wife to read his speeches, but he rarely accepted her suggestions for change. He seemed blind to the implications of many of his statements.

The only speech Lindbergh gave during his appearances at America First rallies in which he mentioned Jews was in Des Moines, Iowa, on September 11, 1941—less than three months before Pearl Harbor. This speech would cause him to be labeled anti-Semitic, a label that would stick.

Anne told me that when she read the draft of his Des Moines speech, she warned her husband that it would be interpreted as a racist attack, but Lindbergh felt that it was not anti-Semitic, simply the truth as he viewed it. And in Des Moines, he called on the Jews of the United States to stop "agitating for war" and to oppose intervention, because the Jews would be the first to feel the consequences when war came.

"Tolerance is a virtue which depends upon peace and strength," Lindbergh warned. He spoke of the vast Jewish influence in the country, especially in the field of communications, and hoped that the Jews, "a race I admire," would not use their influence to "lead our people to destruction."

"I cannot blame people for misinterpreting," Anne Lindbergh told me. "I can understand why the Jews dislike him. There were many times when I wanted him to change his speeches. There were many things I wish Charles had not said." With great distaste, as if she hated the next thought she had to express, she added, "He was tactless. He made blunders."

Why was Charles Lindbergh so reluctant to compromise and change his speeches? His wife must have asked herself this repeatedly, not only in the weeks of public furor that followed the speech, but also in the years to come. When I asked her why her husband was so implacable in presenting his views, she talked about his childhood. His parents, although they did not divorce, lived apart from the time Charles was five. His father maintained a close relationship with his son, but because of his political career he spent much of his time in Washington. Consequently, Charles Lindbergh became unusually self-sufficient and independent when he was still a boy. He was the only "man" on the farm in Little Falls, Minnesota, where he lived with his mother. Nothing in later life would shake the self-confidence he developed then. When he was thirty-eight, he wrote in his diary, "I never trust logical conclusions unless they combine with an inner intuitive feeling, which I find to be really much more reliable. Unless I have this feeling I know with almost complete certainty that my logical reasoning is wrong."

"Charles was not bothered by criticism," Mrs. Lindbergh explained, "because he listened to himself." But in analyzing this truth about her husband, turning it over and over in her mind, Anne Lindbergh characteristically sees that there is another side. She admired her husband's self-confidence and self-awareness, she said. Yet she realized that because of these qualities, when he became convinced he was right, he did not care what others thought. The result was a kind of pride that blinded his perceptions.

Anne Lindbergh never dreamed that one day she would decide to publish her diaries, but the time came when this intensely private woman chose to bare her thoughts and reactions to the years of fame and tragedy—the years from her courtship to the outbreak of World War II; the years which led the Lindberghs, because of their move to Europe and subsequent friendships with pacifists like Lady Astor, to formulate their stand against intervention. She has exposed their naïveté and their idealism. The reader sees the Lindberghs, bright-eyed and enthusiastic, on their trip to Germany to assess Nazi air power; reads of their distress at the reactions of those members of the American press and public who misunderstood the trip; winces at their shortsightedness in not responding to the criticism and failing to explain that the mission was undertaken to provide the United States with needed military intelligence.

In the preface of her prewar diaries, Anne Lindbergh makes an uncharacteristically harsh statement. She claims that she and her husband became the "scapegoats for a generation of failed hopes for peace," when the United States finally entered the war after Pearl Harbor. Just as she is able to see the light and dark sides of her husband's self-confidence, so she can see the positive and negative aspects of hero worship.

"There is tremendous hero worship and devil-baiting in this country," she told me during my second visit with her in Darien. "Devil-baiting is the other side of the coin of hero worship. But that kind of attitude is immature, because one abdicates a sense of responsibility. Something or someone becomes all good or all evil.

"Lots of people were against the war. It makes one despair," she said in obvious frustration, "not knowing how to make people aware of the circumstances, the facts of the controversy." But when I asked if she planned to publish her diaries covering the America First years, she shook her head. "Probably not," she said.

Anne Lindbergh, who is so consumed by the need for honest relations between people and for honest written expression, finds those years and that controversy particularly painful. There is something beyond pain though that prevents her from publishing those diaries: her loyalty to her husband. She is unwilling to air the disagreements she and her husband may have had on the wording of some of his speeches, or on his hasty reaction to Franklin Roosevelt's attack on his patriotism (Charles resigned his commission in the air reserves), or on his refusal to communicate with the media.

A few months before her husband died, a book entitled *Charles Lindbergh and the Battle Against American Intervention in World War II* was published. "It has taken thirty years for a book like this to be published," Mrs. Lindbergh said. "The author doesn't agree with my husband's stands, but he does not question his integrity." She referred to the book in checking a date for me, and I noticed there were at least twenty bits of paper in it, marking various passages. "It is the first objective historical account," she said. "I am grateful that my husband could read it before he died."

The matter of integrity is important to Anne Lindbergh. She insists that her husband abhorred prejudice of any kind, including racial prejudice. She does not ask that people agree with him on everything he said or did, but simply that they do not question his integrity. But she is not a woman to spend her life tilting at windmills. She will not pursue the battle for her husband's honor until her own death. Her only part in the battle now is to hope for perspective. The final assessment of Charles Lindbergh's role before and during World War II is out of her hands and in the hands of historians.

She wrote a letter to me six weeks after my father's resignation which reveals something of her philosophy of dealing with controversy. "I feel I must say one thing to you. I hope you will remember always that you are and will be far into the future, a living witness for your father whether or not you are a speaking witness—just as I feel that our children are and will be living witnesses for my husband, long after his death and mine." She and her children need not take up the gauntlet at each challenge. Facing life and living it in the light of what they have learned from Charles Lindbergh is all that is required. All that matters.

The years have taught Anne Lindbergh to accept the concept of the "living witness" and to believe that perspective may come. But it was difficult for her to live through the months after Pearl Harbor. Charles Lindbergh's opposition to the war was not easily forgotten. Thirteen days after the attack on Pearl Harbor, he tried to enlist in the Army Air Corps, but Secretary of War Stimson refused to give him a commission. After that his civilian services were turned down by Pan American, United Aircraft and Curtiss-Wright. Finally, Lindbergh went to work for Henry Ford. Since the bombers Ford was turning out at the huge Willow Run plant were desperately needed, he had no fears that he would lose any government contracts by hiring Charles Lindbergh. The Lindberghs moved to Detroit in 1942.

Anne Lindbergh felt the effects of their prewar political stand in a different but equally harsh way. The critical reaction to *The Wave of the Future* shook her confidence as a writer. One of the questions uppermost in my mind had been why there was such a long gap between her 1944 novel, *The Steep Ascent,* and her best-selling *Gift from the Sea,* published in 1955. I said I assumed that it was because of the demands of raising five children, but Mrs. Lindbergh's answer was unexpected.

"Yes," she said, "I was busy with the children, but also I was very upset. So upset that I did not want to go on writing." *The Wave of the Future,* which she had thought of as her "confession of faith," had been branded pro-Nazi by many critics, even though she had called the Communists and Nazis "scum riding the waves of the future." Looking back, Anne sees her book as "a pacifist document, and I can understand why it was misinterpreted because it was not a clear document," she told me. "But my reaction at the time was that if I expressed myself so poorly, I should not continue writing."

She explained that while *The Steep Ascent* was published in 1944, she had written most of it before 1939, before *The Wave of the Future.* She described it as a "fictional account of an actual incident" in her own life. It is a sensitively written story of a woman who comes close to death on a flight across the Alps and, in the moment of greatest danger, rediscovers the joys of life. "In a way," she told me, "you would say it was a comeback book." Although she was still hurt by her failure to communicate in *The Wave of the Future*, she had wanted to prove to herself that she still could write. But the reviews were indifferent and the sales were disappointing. It would be another decade before she decided to publish again.

And so she turned to a different art—and a different group of people. While Charles Lindbergh tested bombers at high altitudes, she became involved with the professors and students at Cranbrook Academy of Art, where she studied sculpture. "It was wordless. It gave me another vision," she said. And she made lasting friends there, some of whom she still sees.

The years immediately after the war, she told me, were the most difficult of their marriage. Her husband had spent the last year of the war in the Pacific, testing fighter planes and flying over fifty combat missions. When peace came, like hundreds of thousands of other men, he had to adjust abruptly to civilian life. No longer was he living the high-intensity existence of sacrifice, adventure and duty. No longer was he poised close to death. And Anne had her own adjustments to make when they left Detroit and moved to Connecticut. She missed the stimulation of the artist colony at Cranbrook and her friends there.

They saw very few people in Connecticut. "My husband was very unsocial, really," Anne said. And he began to travel a great deal—alone. With five children ranging in age from one to thirteen, Anne was needed at home. "It was not easy when he was gone, but when he returned he brought a stimulus to the marriage," she said. "In those years I was learning to be a person on my own but it's a hard process."

We talked about marriage and the seemingly unavoidable mistake of expecting more of the one you love than of others, expecting them to meet your needs effortlessly, to share your goals. Reflecting on her own relationship, she told me, "I learned that the partners bring different things to a marriage." She believes that one must accept the loved one just as he is and that the pain two people experience and the mistakes they make when their lives are enmeshed are not defeats or failures to be erased and forgotten. "Only two real people can meet," she wrote in *Dearly Beloved,* more than thirty years after her wedding day. "It had taken years to strip away the illusions, the poses, the pretenses . . . and this was why . . . you could never regret the past, call it a waste or wipe it out."

She wrote most eloquently about honesty in relationships and of what she had learned in her own search for independence in *Gift from the Sea.* It was an immediate success. It spoke to millions of women. Her editors had been worried that it would not sell. They thought a livelier title might help and suggested the well-known quotation from Thoreau "The mass of men lead lives of quiet desperation." Anne Lindbergh agreed that her book does have a note of desperation, but she rejected the suggestion. *Gift from the Sea* is more than a chronicle of search and of occasional discouragement. Anne Lindbergh writes of the patience and faith in oneself that are required in the journey toward independence. She stressed independence because "we are all in the last analysis alone."

She argued that in order to be more complete and whole, men should learn to develop personal relationships and become more inward-looking, women should become more self-sufficient, and both learn to accept impermanence—in relationships with friends, with children, even in marriage. First love is not forever. There comes a time when one fails to note that "this is our fourteenth-month anniversary." A man and a woman move apart because of different needs. Anne Lindbergh stresses the need for "lightness of touch" with those one loves. The phrase is part of the skillful web of images she has woven to describe love and marriage. But I have found that the "fluidity," the "evolution" and especially the "lightness of touch" she speaks of repeatedly often do not fit the realities of marriage.

"Can you really achieve lightness of touch in marriage?" I asked her.

"No, no, of course you can't," she answered eagerly, sympathetically. She thought for a moment and added, speaking more slowly, "Perhaps you shouldn't. Because you love and you care deeply."

Ever honest and willing to have someone question even a cherished concept, Anne Lindbergh agreed that lightness of touch was not always possible. Perhaps what she was trying to express with this phrase is better stated in her poem *Even*.

> Him that I love, I wish to be
> free . . .
> Even from me.

There is a small gray building in the back yard of her house in Darien that looks out of place. It is Anne Lindbergh's writing retreat, an old toolshed that she and her husband found years ago on Route 1. When the Lindberghs moved to Darien, Anne had no quiet place where she could write and think with five children in the house. The toolshed became her haven and an important part of her own journey toward independence.

It is here that she worked on *Gift from the Sea*. Driftwood that Anne picked up on the beach decorates the crossbeams of the little house. There is one long shelf of books, most of them full of bits of paper marking various sections, and above the shelf hangs a cross of unusually beautiful cork, another treasure from the sea. Mexican pottery and three small Indian rugs add color to the otherwise austere room. Her desk

faces the wall. She can see the cove that she loves only
when she leans back in her chair. I was surprised by
the size of her desk. No more than two or three books
and a sheet of paper can be spread out on it, but a
small basket filled with pencils, every one of them
worn down almost to the eraser, was evidence that it
was a working area.

She seemed quiet, a bit wistful when she showed me
her little house. There was a hot plate with a kettle on
it and a curtained-off corner with a wash basin and
toilet so that she could spend the entire day in her
studio if she desired, but from the cobwebs and the
film of dust over everything, including the top of the
desk, it was clear that she had not been working there
lately. When I asked her why, she replied that there
had been just too many requests, too many details of
her husband's estate to attend to, and plans for his
posthumous "Book of Values" that demanded her
attention. She had not been able to snatch more than
fifteen or twenty minutes a day for herself. Not enough
time to write. She had not even written in her diary for
more than three months.

It was not until I had left Darien that I realized
Anne Lindbergh does not need the little toolshed any
more. There are no children at home in need of attention. No household pressures. No need to juggle her
roles as mother, wife and writer. The small gray building serves no real purpose—except as a symbol of her
journey toward independence—now that she is alone.

Charles Lindbergh died of lymphatic cancer in August, 1974, at their home in Maui, Hawaii. He had
not been well since the autumn of 1973, but the
doctors did not diagnose his illness as cancer until the
following July. He prepared for his death naturally
and calmly, with the precision and courage with which
he undertook the dangerous pioneering flights of his
youth. Eight days before he died, he asked to be flown
to Maui. Once there, he put his personal papers in
order, made arrangements for his coffin, and planned

what he would wear for burial. "He was so human and natural about it," their daughter Reeve told me. "I was never prouder of him than in his death."

Anne Lindbergh did not want to talk about those last days in Hawaii, but she did tell me that she hopes eventually to write about widowhood and about "our unwillingness to face death, to meet it."

She is meeting it now. Meeting it every day as she drinks from the dark blue china mug with "Charles" on it. She meets it at night by reading philosophy. A favorite book is *How I Believe* by Catholic theologian Pierre Teilhard de Chardin. "I always carry books with me. I have to have them to get to sleep," she said. And she needs them because she is now embarked on "the final lesson of learning to be independent—widowhood." She told me that "it is the hardest lesson of all." It is the lesson of learning how to see and do familiar things without the familiar person by your side to react, to laugh with, to listen.

Anne Lindbergh and I took a walk across an open field near her house, a walk she and her husband took so often together, a walk she now takes by herself almost every afternoon. It was spring, almost summer, and just a few days before her seventieth birthday. She seemed young, however, in her pink blouse and wrap-around skirt and tennis shoes—field glasses slung around her neck to observe the birds. We followed a track across the field toward the trees and then a path through the woods that led to a small pond.

Despite the many times that she has walked through this field and along these paths, there was nothing ordinary about them to Anne Lindbergh. She pointed out each new growth, each change in color. Her scruffy-looking cairn terrier and a neighbor's German shepherd kept us company, racing ahead as if the field were an exciting new adventure for them as well.

The walk evoked memories of her husband and emotions that Anne Lindbergh wanted to share. "It is very difficult—so very difficult to be alone," she told me. As she said this, she seemed very self-contained, certainly not a fragile flower that could not survive if uprooted. And so I was slightly startled when she confided in a low voice, "I still feel married." She added quickly, "I feel marriage goes on. I don't say this in some Ouija-board sense, but in the way you approach things, see things, always aware of how your husband would approach them, see them." She spoke earnestly as if asking, "You *do* understand what I mean?"

The Lindberghs shared a delight in the beauty of nature and found it no matter where they lived—the New Jersey countryside, an island off the coast of Brittany, in Paris and in Detroit. "Invisible things (of nature) speak to him, cry out, as people's emotions do to me," Anne wrote in her diary a few years after they were married. "It is quite exciting and he teaches me to see."

That walk, even without Charles Lindbergh, was a release for Anne. For as long as she can remember, nature has comforted her. I asked her why. The question seemed to surprise her. After a moment she answered carefully, "I find the cycle of nature very comforting—death in winter, rebirth in spring." When she was depressed, she said, "I would go outside and sometimes just walk around and around and say, 'Just what is it that you love? New grass? A bird?' Even in college I would go off alone and sit on a stump and think."

A few days after our walk, Anne Lindbergh wrote me, "There were so many unfinished threads." She wanted me to know that nature is a constant flow in her life, not a resource to be drawn upon only when disheartened. "I do like to go out and sit under a tree," she wrote, "or on an overturned boat with my bird glasses. A moment of quiet before the day starts—to pray—to feel myself one with nature before the inevitable desk work and telephone calls. It helps me to decide which are the most important things to do that day. (And I do it in the evening as well, if I can, which helps me to accept the things I have not done!)"

Her relationship with her husband makes me think of the words to a song by Simon and Garfunkel— "The only truth I know is you." His death must leave an awful void in her life. Although she had spent years learning to be independent and seems to be facing widowhood squarely now, for most of her marriage and perhaps even to the end, the practical, purposeful aspects of life were centered in her husband. In a sense, Charles Lindbergh was the strongest grip she had on life. And she knew this. Ten years after they were married, she wrote that only her husband's "technical ability and the children fit me into this world." Her world was one of poetry and ideas. When one reads her diaries, she often seems not to be a creature of this world. She is too sensitive, too poetic, too caught up in search of what she has described as "different planes of existence . . . *La vie triviale, la vie tragique.*"

Her husband recognized this other-world quality in Anne. In his journals he described the birth of their fifth child. During labor, Anne had propped up on her bedside table a postcard reproduction of a centuries-old American Indian sculpture, a wooden deer head with seashell eyes. The postcard represented something to Anne "that is beyond life and beyond this world in a sense, just as Anne holds that same element herself," Charles wrote. "She uses it as a bridge and on it crosses into a world beyond our own—a world to which she belongs more than anyone I have ever known. Anne always seems to me to stand on life and, at the same time, touch something beyond it. Yet her ability to touch beyond does not cause her to relinquish life any more than her ability to live restricts the unlimited travels of her spirit."

She loved flying because from the air she felt outside of life. Magically, she could look in. And writing gave her similar power. She was alone, guiding her pen across a piece of paper. In control.

Her fears made it difficult for Anne Lindbergh to fit into this world. Something irreplaceable had been torn from her—her firstborn—and she feared loving too much, feared the unknown. The candor of her prose and poetry, her openness even about her fight against depression, is extraordinary—a vivid contrast to her apparent fear of interviewers and her reluctance to express her thoughts to them, as if only she could interpret her private world to the larger world outside.

She still needs time in her private world. When I visited her she mentioned that she cannot write, cannot think if she is inundated with visitors and telephone calls. She is incapable of working on correspondence with her part-time secretary unless she has time beforehand to think about each letter and mull an answer over in her mind.

All her life she has fought an almost abnormal shyness, the kind that "can freeze your face and tongue, paralyze the muscles in your jaw, paralyze your limbs, too, so that you cannot walk into a room or speak or even smile." I had the feeling that she was still fighting that shyness, although she seems to genuinely enjoy contact with others. When she told me about the pioneer surveying flights with her husband in the first years of their marriage, one of the adjustments she mentioned having to make was, "I liked different things. I liked people. I was terribly interested in the people in those faraway places." Yet there were many times when she liked people, but liked her own world more.

During that terrible year of testing when she had to deal with the anguish caused by the Hauptmann trial as well as that caused by the death of her older sister Elisabeth, she wrote, "I realize I avoid people because people mean so much to me. They throw me off keel so easily." And she was married to a man who avoided contact with most people. Anne Lindbergh could easily have become reclusive and withdrawn into her own world. But she broke through her fears and shyness because, despite her fragile sensitivity, she wanted to "live consciously."

Reeve Lindbergh Brown by chance captured a vignette of her mother in a movie she was taking of her first child. It was not until Reeve viewed the developed film that she realized what a revealing and beautiful moment she had recorded. Reeve and her husband had been spending a few days with her parents at Scott's Cove. It was the end of the day, a cool fall evening. Reeve filmed her little girl playing with her grandfather. Then Charles Lindbergh, bundled up in a lumber jacket against the chill, started to walk toward the woods. He was a solitary figure, his head down. Reeve could not help thinking that her father seemed old and slightly stooped. She knew he was ill, but she could not know that this was the last year of his life.

Almost out of film, Reeve decided to finish the roll with a few scenes of Scott's Cove in the sunset. She found her mother standing at the water's edge throwing handfuls of cracked corn to the birds. Reeve simply let the film run until there was no more. In those moments as she filmed, she was acutely conscious of all the worries burdening her mother—the pain of seeing her husband's strength and spirit weakened by illness, the dismay and impotence she felt over a soon-to-be-published biography that would reinforce the old anti-democratic and pro-Nazi image of her husband.

"All these things were going on in her life," Reeve said, "and yet she was there, feeding the birds—always nourishing others, yet always alone and private. I wanted to help her, to say something. But I realized that although she was very much alone, there was something wonderful about her aloneness. It was not the aloneness of being wounded or not being able to communicate or touch others. But aloneness in the sense of being all right and intact.

"She always meets life. She faces everything. Even now I cry when I watch that film."

Reeve's portrait of her mother in the midst of pain, still able to give and to nourish, helped me understand more fully a theme that runs through Anne Lindbergh's writings: you have to let go of life and it is given back to you. "Life is a gift, given in trust—like a child." This perception of life as a gift has made it precious to Anne Lindbergh. It has given her the courage to try to live as the heroine of *The Steep Ascent*—"Not to be hurried, not to be afraid, not to be imprisoned in one's self. To be open, aware, vulnerable—even to fear, even to pain, even to death." And not to be imprisoned by images or futile battles against them.

When Anne Lindbergh drove me to the train station after my last visit with her, we sat in her brown Pinto station wagon as we waited the remaining few minutes for my 4:40 train back to New York City. We were talking about Charles Lindbergh and his most recent biographer's assessment of him as a totalitarian because of his views on World War II. "One must wait for perspective," she said. "They say it will come eventually, but I am not sure."

She spoke matter of factly, almost without expression. I felt that she could face the probability that her perception of her husband would never be widely shared. We spoke briefly of my own father and the question of perspective on his life. There was much more I wanted to say, but the train was coming into the station. I had to cross the parking area and go up the stairs to the platform. There was only time to say good-bye.

I wanted to give her a quick hug, but I did not. Even at that moment, she was very much a controlled, private person, a person of strength. So instead, I took her hand and squeezed it.

On the way back to New York as I went over my notes and filled in the gaps, I reread a letter Reeve had written me about her mother's adjustment to widowhood. "She weathers everything and comes out whole," she had written, "she is the strongest person I know. We all worry about her constantly but she is, in fact, invincible." As I read those words, I was especially glad that despite Anne's eleven years of publishing silence, she had weathered that battle as well. Grateful, too, that she had softened her 1936 judgment that "writing is taking . . . and not giving."

I knew she had spoken recently at the commencement of her eldest grandchild and had told the graduates that when she was in college, she had confided to a friend, "To me the most exciting thing in life is communication," and that looking back over her life, she still believed those words. Her belief enabled Anne Lindbergh to overcome her fears and the restricting images that prohibited growth. It enabled her to resist withdrawing too much into her other world.

There is a Benedictine monastery a few hours' drive from Darien. Anne and Charles Lindbergh first went there several years ago to attend a seminar on conservation. They returned for other visits. Now Anne occasionally makes the journey alone. She likes to go, because "I have no image there . . . I am a naked soul." Her words did not surprise me. The monastery offers privacy for a sensitive woman who values above all else honesty and truth.

And perhaps its peace strengthens her so that she can continue to give her children not happiness, for that is impossible, but clues to life—the clues she wrote about in *Dearly Beloved:* "A thread of perception, a crack of light, a key to the open door." For her children, for me, and for many of those who have read her books, these gifts have been sufficient.

Mao
Tse-
tung

"Ten thousand years is too long.
Seize the day! Seize the hour!"

ON NEW YEAR'S EVE, 1975, my husband and I watched the clock pass twelve in the presence of Chairman Mao Tse-tung, the revolutionary leader of China's 800 million people. This was to be the last New Year of his life.* It was one of the most extraordinary moments of ours.

We sat in Mao's study, deep within the Forbidden City where he dwelt, as he had once told André Malraux, "alone with the masses." The Chairman was no remote, godlike figure, but an old man, his body humbled by illness, but still alert, unselfconscious and seemingly eager to talk with us. There were times that midnight when it was difficult to remember that this frail, elderly man, who enjoyed his interpreter's gentle teasing, had once been the young revolutionist who had exhorted his comrades to "trample the beds of rich men's daughters."

We were the second to last Americans to visit Mao Tse-tung. Our visit came about through an odd combination of circumstances, more by chance than by plan. In September of 1975, a friend of ours from the 1968 Presidential campaign days wrote from Peking, where he was visiting American Ambassador George

---

* Both the Chinese New Year, which falls in February, and the Western New Year are observed in the People's Republic of China. *The People's Daily*, the country's daily newspaper, customarily ran a full-page portrait of Chairman Mao on January 1 to mark the holiday.

Bush, about the four weeks he had just spent traveling in China. He reported that so many of the people he had met had mentioned my father's 1972 trip and his initiative in establishing relations with the People's Republic that he was certain the Chinese would welcome a visit from us.

It was out of the question, of course. But David would have three weeks off between his law school semesters at the end of the year, and the more we thought about the outlandish idea of taking those three weeks to fly 7,500 miles in the dead of winter to a country we had never dreamed of visiting, the more tempting it became. A week later I called my father in San Clemente and asked if he could help us obtain a visa by getting in touch with Ambassador Huang-chen, the head of the Chinese Liaison Office in Washington. I knew the Ambassador had paid a friendship call on my father only a month earlier. Less than twenty-four hours later, David and I received an invitation to visit China as the personal guests of the Ambassador.

The rest of that fall was busy, taken up with work, law school and several visits to the Chinese Liaison Office to arrange the details of our trip—where we would go, what we should see. We requested the opportunity to deliver personally letters of greeting from my father to Chairman Mao and, if his health permitted, Premier Chou En-lai, whom we had heard was suffering from cancer. We were told that all our inquiries were being forwarded to Peking. The officials at the Liaison Office in Washington were very correct and maintained a strict posture of reticence about our itinerary. Right up to the moment of our departure we were uncertain of where we would be going and what we would see—or whom we would meet.

In early December, soon after President Ford's return from Peking, the Chinese had inquired whether we had any objections to "meeting our leaders alone" —meaning without any members of the American Mission in Peking being present. This was a hint that our trip was regarded as more than a simple courtesy extended to us in acknowledgement of my father's 1972 initiative, but at the time we attached no significance to it, since we were going to China as private citizens and had had no contact with the State Department.

Not until we actually landed in Peking at one in the morning of December 29 did we suspect that there was a greater interest in our visit (and a greater power behind it) than that of the anonymous officials of the Chinese Foreign Ministry. As our plane taxied to a stop, we looked out the window and saw six or seven people walking toward the plane. It looked like a greeting party. I was surprised that so many people would come out to the airport at one in the morning. It was a bitterly cold night and they were all so bundled up that I could not tell if they were men or women. But as we came down the steps, I recognized Nancy Tang. She had appeared in many photographs of my father's trip to China three years earlier. Nancy was Mao's personal interpreter. Ambassador Huang-chen was there, too. He and his wife had flown from Washington to Peking earlier that month.

After brief introductions, the Ambassador escorted us to a luxurious government guesthouse instead of to a hotel as we had expected. I knew that only people on official business were honored with guesthouse accommodations. And ours were truly magnificent. The guesthouse was the former Austro-Hungarian Embassy, a columned mansion with bullet holes in the walls from the Boxer Rebellion—and bathrooms larger than the kitchen in our Washington apartment.

It was now clear to David and me that our trip was destined to be far from routine. But we still did not dream that forty-six hours after our arrival we would be summoned for a private visit with Chairman Mao Tse-tung.

"We don't want you to be alone on New Year's Eve," Ambassador and Madame Huang-chen had said

155

as they invited us to a small dinner party in our honor in the guesthouse. Despite the Chinese custom of dining early, our New Year's Eve dinner did not start until nine. It was leisurely, and we lingered at the table until I was afraid that I would fall asleep. At eleven, explaining how tired I was, I ended the evening.

Ten minutes later, when we were back in our bedroom, there was a knock at the door. Already in my nightgown, I hid behind the wardrobe while David went to see who it was. The Protocol Officer excitedly announced, "Chairman Mao would like to see you." It did not seem necessary to ask how soon the car would arrive. I changed as quickly as I could back into the dress I had worn to dinner, and as I put it on I was very grateful to my mother. David and I had spent Christmas at San Clemente and as I was packing for our trip to China, my mother asked if I had a long-sleeved dress to wear in the evening. "You need one," she said. "The Chinese dress very modestly." I had nothing suitable, so she let me borrow one of her dresses—a dark flowered print, long and very soft, one of those dresses you can roll up in a ball in the bottom of your suitcase and not have to worry about wrinkles. I remember looking for my watch so I could note the exact time of our meeting, and as we left our room, I carefully carried the manila envelope containing the letter from my father to Chairman Mao.

The night was freezing cold as David and I were driven through Peking, alone in the back seat of a black Chinese-made limousine very much like a Rolls-Royce. We were enclosed in the heavy tank-like car by a cocoon of black net curtains that covered all the windows except the driver's windshield. The only vehicles on the streets, apart from Ambassador Huang-chen's limousine, which followed us, were horse-drawn wooden carts filled with farm produce, and some military jeeps and trucks. We rode in silence through the labyrinth of streets in the old part of Peking. No lights shone in the dark and as we passed mile after mile of walled city, we were acutely aware of being very much on our own, cut off from everything familiar.

At a checkpoint, guarded by People's Liberation Army soldiers, the car swung through a gate into the Forbidden City. Suddenly out of the black, a huge, brilliantly lighted billboard loomed up in front of us. In Chairman Mao's calligraphy, it bore his injunction "Serve the people." We swerved left almost immediately onto the winding lakeside road that led to Mao's house. Later, when I saw a Chinese newsreel of our visit, I realized that the billboard was brightly lighted so that the television cameras could film the arrival of our car. The front of the Chairman's house was also lighted for television. The abrupt change from the darkness we had been driving through to the glare of the high-intensity lights almost blinded me. I was able to discern only the bare outline of the modest, one-story house we were entering.

But it was not only the late hour and the sudden burst of blinding light that disoriented me. It was also the strangeness of being in an alien world and my awe that we were about to meet the leader whom millions of people considered more god than man.

We realized later that there had been clues to our midnight visit, clues that we had failed to pick up. One of the Ambassador's aides had been called to the telephone four separate times during the dinner party earlier. And the night before, the Vice Foreign Minister had remarked rather pointedly, "I understand you want to meet our leaders." Then, too, the schedule of that day, our third in China, had read, "Evening of December 31, OPEN."

A single attendant, dressed in a Mao suit like all the other Chinese officials we met, opened the door. He took our coats and those of Ambassador Huang-chen and the Foreign Minister. There was no conversation. Another man came forward to welcome us formally to Mao's private home. I recognized him. He was China's Chief of Protocol, who had escorted us to our meeting with the Foreign Minister the day before. Now he hurriedly ushered us from the small reception area into a dark room, just large enough for the Ping-Pong table and three or four wooden chairs we could distinguish in the gloom. A door at the other end of the room opened onto a lighted room beyond.

We walked quickly through the dark Ping-Pong room, and, as we crossed the threshold into the light, I saw Mao Tse-tung. He was sunk into an enormous, slipcovered easy chair, one of six identical chairs arranged in a semicircle in his study. My first impression was of a tired old man with vacant eyes, his jaw slack.

The Chairman struggled to his feet with the help of two young women dressed alike in gray Mao suits. Once on his feet, he tottered for a moment, and then the women stepped back and he stood alone. I sensed a stir behind us. A television cameraman and an assistant holding lights had slipped into the room. The cameraman photographed the Chairman as he leaned forward and gave first me, and then David, a firm handshake. Then they were gone as quickly and silently as they had appeared.

The Chief of Protocol motioned for me to sit next to the Chairman. I sat well forward in the huge chair. If I had sat back, my feet would have been several inches off the floor. After two days of intensive, non-stop lectures from workers, soldiers, peasants, Party members and Foreign Ministry officials, I expected similar homilies from Chairman Mao. Consequently, while his attendants were helping him back into his chair, I relaxed and looked around the stark room. There was no luxury here—floor-to-ceiling shelves filled with looseleaf books and scrolls, strange six-foot-high lamps with high-intensity bulbs for television, wooden tables between the armchairs with cylinder-shaped tins of Panda cigarettes (Mao had the reputation of being a chainsmoker, but he did not smoke during our visit), delicate porcelain cups of green tea, and small lacquered trays containing rolled-up washcloths—warm and wet

—to wipe our fingers. Beneath each table, a white spit-toon. I had discovered the day before that spitting was a socially acceptable custom when we met with a high official and, right in the middle of a sentence, he cleared his throat and used the spittoon between my chair and his.

Once Mao was settled into his chair, I found it difficult to look closely at him. Despite my eagerness to meet the Chairman, now that we were actually in his presence I felt it was somehow an intrusion to see him this way. His jaw hanging down—obviously the result of a stroke—gave him a vacant look. His yellow skin seemed almost translucent. It had a waxlike texture and was almost totally unlined. His immaculate Mao suit, gray just like those of his attendants, hung loosely on his body. His long arms and large hands seemed dead weights dangling at his sides. And when he spoke, the sounds emerged as grunts—harsh, primitive, la-bored.

I took my father's letter out of the manila envelope that I had been carrying and gave it to Mao. He handed it to Nancy Tang, his interpreter, and she im-mediately set to work translating it for the Chairman.

During the three days she had spent with us since meeting us at the airport, we had found Brooklyn-born Nancy Tang to be a pleasant companion—and an un-yielding Maoist. She had lived in New York until she was six years old, but she dismissed the United States as a country that "expects people to accept their lot in life." Nancy's hair was severely bobbed and she wore steel-rimmed glasses, but she looked young and seemed completely at ease as she sat next to the Chair-man. When she translated Mao's words to us, she fre-quently consulted with the other two interpreters, who sat behind her on straight-backed chairs, to determine exactly what the Chairman had said. His speech was evidently unclear from time to time. After each quick conference, she would repeat Mao's words back to him before translating them for us. If she had not conveyed his thought precisely, Mao would grunt corrections and tap his fingers on Nancy's notebook. The interplay between Nancy and Mao was bantering at moments. She seemed almost playful as she submitted to his corrections. I sensed a hint of coquetry. There was a warm rapport between the aged revolutionary and his thirty-two-year-old interpreter, striking in this purposely and starkly asexual society.

It was not until my father's letter had been translated that I realized how very much in control and mentally alert Chairman Mao really was. He seemed pleased by my father's personal message and said very emphatically, "Mr. Nixon is welcome in China." (A month later my parents would meet with Mao Tse-tung in the Forbidden City.) Then he took my father's letter from Nancy's hand and, to my astonishment, distinctly and precisely read the date at the top of the letter, "December 23, 1975," out loud in English. It was an effective way of telling us that his physical handicap had not affected his mental agility.

Mao informed me that the chair I was sitting in was the same one my father had used during his visit almost four years earlier. I told the Chairman I would like to switch places with David so he could say that he too had occupied an historic seat. As we made the quick change, Mao laughed heartily. Then he asked, "How is Mr. Nixon's leg?" David launched into a description of the effects of phlebitis. When I saw that Mao was looking straight ahead and not at David or me, I uneasily thought that David might be telling the Chairman more than he wanted to know. But as our visit progressed, I discovered that he rarely looked in our direction, but instead concentrated his attention on the interpreters.

It was an extremely warm and friendly meeting. I showed the Chairman that I was wearing a small pin bearing his profile that the Ambassador's wife had given me. Though Mao had seen literally millions of men and women wearing similar tin medals, he reacted with a childlike delight and impulsively clasped my hand.

Mao had an unexpected gentleness—perhaps because of his age and the humbling dependence on others for basic needs which comes with illness. He did not posture. He spoke self-deprecatingly about a poem on struggle which would be published to mark the New Year. "It is nothing," he said, "I wrote it in 1965."

I found it impossible not to compare his attitude with that of other all-powerful dictators I had met. I thought especially of Brezhnev, who often spoke in a conspiratorial, melodramatic whisper so that his audience had to hang on to every word. Brezhnev enjoyed clapping his hands while people laughed and smiled on cue. And visiting Greece's Papadapoulos had seemed almost like a parody of an old movie. He received us, seated behind a huge fortress-like desk, in a room sixty by thirty feet. Visitors were given low chairs to assure they would listen in an attitude of proper respect. In contrast, within the Forbidden City, Mao and Nancy interacted as grandfather and granddaughter. Ambassador Huang-chen appeared relaxed and gazed casually around the room. I was surprised when he did not lean forward in his chair to catch every word the Chairman spoke.

Mao Tse-tung was the first person we had met in China who dropped the pretense that the People's Republic is a utopian, perfect society. He actually sounded skeptical, almost disappointed in his people, especially the young. "Young people are soft," he said to us. "They have to be reminded of the need for struggle." At this he became animated, like a young man, for the first time during our visit. Vigorously, he jabbed his forefingers together to emphasize the need for struggle. Struggle was more than just a word for Mao, it was the underlying principle of his philosophy. "There will be struggle in the Party. There will be struggle between the classes. Nothing is certain except struggle," he told us.

Then suddenly he asked, "What do you think?"

His question was so unexpected that both David and I hesitated. Then we spoke at the same moment. "I agree . . ." Our voices were hollow echoes of each other. There was a silence as Mao waited for us to say more. Finally he spoke again, "It is quite possible the struggle will last for two or three hundred years."

It was very moving to witness the effort of this old man as he spoke of struggle. A whole country turned to the little red book of Mao's quotations whenever they felt in need of strength. But, I wondered to whom and to what did the Chairman turn in moments of doubt.

I was surprised that he made no effort to hide how keenly he sensed his mortality. When he spoke of the future, he spoke of a future out of his control. I remembered that he had once rated the chance of permanent success for his revolution at less than fifty percent.

The Long March, that now almost mythical 368 days, had tested and strengthened his generation, but now they were almost all dead. It worried him that he had to depend on this new generation, which had never experienced insurrection and war, to continue the struggle. Against the weight of history, he asked them to carry on the revolution to achieve a perfect class-less society. "For thousands of years it was said that . . . it was wrong to rebel. Marxism changed that," Mao told Chinese youth.

As Mao spoke of struggle, I felt that in spite of the infirmities of age, he was more dedicated to struggle than the young Chinese we had met and talked with.

After this burst of energy, Mao was silent. Then, as if responding to a question he often posed to himself, he described how he had dealt with his opponents in the past. "We are not terrible. We recognize that people commit errors. And if they understand their errors, they are fully restored to their former positions." Then, defensively, as though seeking our approval, he said, "We don't shoot people." After a pause, he added, "We forgave several Nationalists the other day." He was referring to the release of some Nationalist soldiers who had fought the Communists during the civil war. It was clear that Mao was sincere in his fervent belief that man could be reformed. I wondered, however, if he was conscious also of the irony of his statement. There had been no attempt to reeducate all of those, some say as many as 26,000,000, who had perished in resisting the Red Chinese.

The time passed quickly, and around twelve-thirty the Foreign Minister started signaling us from across the room, tapping on his watch to remind us of the lateness of the hour. Twice during the next fifteen minutes, I got up from my chair. And twice the Chairman protested, motioning with both of his hands for us to remain in our seats. Finally we were allowed to say goodnight.

Throughout our visit, I had been fascinated by the two young attendants who sat behind Mao and carefully, even tenderly, watched his every movement. They almost seemed to breathe with him. As we prepared to leave, Mao leaned forward to rise from his chair. One of the girls, swift and graceful despite her bulky Mao suit, ran a comb through his hair so that he would be ready for the television cameras again. She had an extraordinarily serene and beautiful face. And her hair—unlike that of any other woman I saw in China—was softly curled. Her gentle assistance was a reminder that the once physically powerful man was now dependent on a circle of attendants who jealously protected him from stress and helped soften his isolation.

When we said good-bye, there was a firmness and determination in the Chairman's voice as he told me, bringing his arms down heavily on the sides of his chair for emphasis: "When your father comes, I will be waiting." And there was bravado and an air of unreality in Ambassador Huang-chen's assurance as we departed through the Ping-Pong room that the Chairman did not just watch the game, but still enjoyed playing it. And there was a final sad silhouette of Mao in the doorway supported by his two nurses. He was a god to his people and yet a human man who ten years before had said: "Men do not like to bear the burden of the revolution throughout their lives."

Why were David and I given an audience with Chairman Mao on New Year's Eve? Was it because of the personal warmth of the relationship between him and my father? The Chinese speak of my father as a "man ahead of his time," because of his vision of Sino-American relations, and Acting Premier Teng Hsiao-ping told me on New Year's Day, "We have never attached much importance to the Watergate affair." David and I traveled to China on the wave of goodwill created by my father's 1972 trip and his effort to build a bridge across thousands of miles and decades of noncommunication. To the Chinese, the Shanghai Communiqué, which was jointly signed at the end of that trip, is insurance that the People's Republic will not be swallowed up by the Soviet Union.

The day after our meeting with Mao we saw a copy of the English-language news summary that the Chinese distribute to foreigners in Peking and read that the Agence France Presse correspondent George Bianni had written that David and I were accorded "astonishing" treatment, "unprecedented for people without high rank." The Chinese used our visit to send a message to Washington that they wanted the relationship symbolized by the Shanghai Communiqué to continue. At the same time, the Chinese felt that the current United States-Soviet détente was in reality a Soviet victory. Despite his years of diatribes against American "imperialism" in Vietnam, Mao feared that in the aftermath of Vietnam the United States was becoming isolationist. It was fascinating for us to learn as we talked with members of our party that conservative Ronald Reagan was popular in Peking because of his outspoken opposition to the "new isolationists" and to those who favored cuts in defense spending.

We were in China as private tourists without diplomatic passports. And yet the Chinese government was sending us home with an urgent message: Beware the grasping hand of Soviet imperialism. Perhaps they overestimated our ability to spread the word.

On New Year's Day at a luncheon given by Acting Premier Teng Hsiao-ping, David joked about entering politics. One of the hosts said, "We'll vote for you!" A quick calculation of voting-age Chinese meant David would carry the nation, with that kind of backing, by about 478,000,000 votes!

Whatever the reasons for the semi-official nature of our trip, there was a personal element that transcended cold political realities—Mao's attitude toward my father. We witnessed an emotional expression of this in the toast Ambassador Huang-chen gave at the small farewell banquet for David and me in Shanghai.

The Ambassador spoke bitterly of the broken promises of the Soviet Union, of how in 1960 the Soviets cynically abrogated the Sino-Soviet Pact, the pact which Mao had declared ten years earlier was "eternal and indestructible." "Our friendship was torn up like a piece of paper," Huang-chen said.

During the following decade, the rift widened and by the time my father became President in 1969, there was a real possibility that China and Russia would go to war. That was why the Chinese appreciated my father's stern opposition to Soviet "adventurism," whether against China or any other nation. I imagine that Mao also felt a rapport with a President who, despite the risk that the Soviets would cancel the scheduled Summit meeting in Moscow, went ahead with the May, 1972, bombing of Hanoi and the mining of Haiphong Harbor in response to the brutal North Vietnamese offensive, and in an attempt to end the war. Though Mao supported North Vietnam, there were indications later that he respected the determination of the United States to stand by its allies and friends despite Soviet pressure. The bombing was a bold action which won the respect, if not the approval, of a man who was known for his own daring in foreign policy.

The Ambassador ended his toast by recalling my father's words during his visit to San Clemente six months earlier. "When I left office I discovered who my friends really are." The Ambassador's aide had tears in his eyes as he translated Huang's final words for us—"The Chinese do not forget their friends."

The Ambassador's words were moving, but they were also jarring. Mao had liquidated many loyal friends: Kao Kang in 1953; Liu Shao-Ch'i in 1966; Lin Piao, who once extolled Mao as "China's greatest liberator, statesman, teacher, strategist, philosopher, poet laureate and national hero," in 1971. But perhaps this friendship with an American could be idealized because my father was no longer in office. His relationship with China was part of history, unchangeable.

At the end of the farewell banquet, we drank a toast to my father on the eve of his sixty-third birthday. Huang-chen asked that as soon as David and I returned to Washington, we telephone the Chinese Liaison Office to inform them of our safe arrival. "Chairman Mao has followed your trip," he said. "He considers you part of his family."

Despite every effort by Mao and our official hosts to make us feel at ease during our trip, most of the time David and I were in China we felt as if we were on another planet. Our isolation was complete. We did not know the language. We were insulated in government guesthouses or hotels where we ate all our meals with the Ambassador and the four other members of our party—the Ambassador's wife, his aide, a protocol man and the interpreter. The strain was greatest in Peking because the guesthouse there is still used by the Russians during the almost perpetual Sino-Soviet border talks, and we assumed that every inch of it was wired. As a result, we communicated through amateur sign language, facial contortions and double-talk.

In an attempt to maintain our perspective, we set aside what we called "the five minutes" at the end of each day. And we spent those five minutes reflecting on who and where we were—two Americans dropped down in an isolated, xenophobic and humorless society, cut off from the United States, even cut off from daily newspaper information after we left Peking. During those five minutes we would stand at a window at night and look out into a vast darkness, whether in Peking, Canton or Shanghai. By half-past nine, everyone was asleep, and cities the size of Chicago were as dark and quiet as an Appalachian farm except for the towering red neon signs proclaiming the slogans of Mao's revolution, the only steady light over a sleeping population which would arise, expressionless, within eight hours to resume the work of building New China.

There was little to remind us of life in the United States, with one memorable exception. At the zoo in Peking on New Year's Day we not only saw the pandas, but also ran into Representative Margaret Heckler, who was touring China with a group of Congresswomen. She had a copy of *The People's Daily* with the front-page photograph of David and me with the Chairman. "Wait until Bella* sees this!" she said, and rolled her eyes upward. For a moment we were back in Washington.

We were often surprised during those two weeks by the isolation that diplomacy, geography and ideology have imposed on the Chinese. Our host, Ambassador Huang-chen, had been China's representative to the United States since 1973, yet when I asked him what his favorite restaurant was in Washington, I discovered that he had never been in a Washington restaurant.

Our conversations were almost always one-way.

* Representative Bella Abzug of New York.

The Chinese expressed little interest in America or the American way of life. They asked no questions about our life at home. This is not to say that they had not done a tremendous amount of research about us. They knew many details about our families and mentioned that General Eisenhower had visited Shanghai in 1938 with Mamie and their son John. I had brought a small album of snapshots of my family and David's, our vegetable garden in San Clemente and our pets, thinking that these glimpses of our life might interest the Chinese, but they evoked only the mildest polite interest. The only photograph that drew any response was a snapshot of David with his grandfather—the devil incarnate to the Chinese, the man who had pulled the strings that activated the hated John Foster Dulles.

Mao's warmth and reference to his considering us part of his family made me curious to know more about his personal life and especially about his children, but despite my efforts, I learned practically nothing. Mao was a one-dimensional god. His likes and dislikes, his loved ones and friends, were not discussed.

In his determination to supplant Confucian devotion to the family with loyalty to the state, Mao had made it clear that he was not creating a dynasty. There are conflicting accounts about the number of children he had fathered. Edgar Snow, the journalist who had several long interviews with Mao over the years, mentioned two sons born to Mao's second wife and two daughters by the fourth Madame Mao, Chiang Ch'ing. One biographer, Stuart Schram, writes that Mao's third wife, Ho Tzu-chen, bore him five children, including one born on the Long March.

I find it incredible that Mao divorced Ho while in exile in Yenan in order to marry Chiang Ch'ing, for Ho was one of the thirty-one women who survived the legendary six-thousand-mile Long March from southeast China to the mountain fastness of Yenan in the northwest. For one year and three days, the Red

Army, 100,000 strong, retreated from Chiang Kai-shek's Nationalists. They crossed thirty-four rivers and eighteen mountain ranges, scrambling along mountain trails so narrow that men and animals fell off, struggling through mud so deep that many were swallowed up in the mire. Only 15,000 lived to reach Yenan.

The Long March became central to Mao's existence, the most important part of the image he created of his own greatness. He compared the Long March to the creation of the world, asking, "Since Pan Ku [the mythical creator of the world] divided the heaven from the earth . . . has history ever witnessed a Long March such as ours?" And yet he eliminated from his life the woman who had shared this ordeal with him. It was as if he alone could comprehend the agony, he alone could be the ultimate symbol, the veteran of the Long March.

Even in his fourth marriage, Mao still cultivated the image of standing alone, godlike, with total focus on duty to the state. Chiang Ch'ing's identity was not tied to his. She became a public figure in her own right as the leader of the radical faction during the Cultural Revolution.

The other members of his family were invisible, with the exception of his niece, Wang Hai-jung, who at thirty-four was the Vice Foreign Minister. But she kept her identity separate from Mao's. Once we asked her how she was related to the Chairman. All she said, in cold dismissal, was, "Some people say that I am related." Every time I asked about Mao's family I met the same dismissal, the same closed door.

The only glimpses of the Chairman's human side come from his writings. Mao's early writings provide flashes of the man of flesh and blood. In 1919, after the suicide of a young woman whose parents had forced her into a traditional marriage, Mao wrote nine articles in thirteen days, passionately denouncing the old society and calling for the "great wave of the freedom to love." There are 57,000,000 copies of

Mao's poetry in print, roughly equivalent to all the volumes of English-language poets in print since the invention of the printing press. His poem *Tapoti* gives the reader insight into a man who could describe sunlight and shadows on a mountain as

Red, orange, yellow, green, blue, violet, indigo:
Who is dancing with these rainbow colors in the sky?

and in the next lines stun—with hard revolutionary realism:

Bullet holes in village walls.
These mountain passes are decorated,
Looking even more beautiful today.

Chinese rulers have always written poetry, but Mao's poetry seems more of a personal indulgence than a bow to tradition. He wrote in classical characters that the average Chinese could not understand. He had stated publicly that poetry, however revolutionary in theme, was not healthy for young minds. Yet he allowed "unproletarian" praise of his works. It seems evident that Mao wanted to believe his poetry was a useful vehicle for dramatizing political messages.

On New Year's Day, 1976, in full knowledge of his mortality, Mao used poetry to call for renewed struggle and to issue another warning against the Soviet Union. When we read *The People's Daily* only hours after our meeting with the Chairman, the impact of his words to us about struggle and revolution was dramatically reinforced by the poems that appeared beneath the large photograph of the Chairman greeting us (it was the first time in fifteen years that he had not appeared alone in his New Year's Day portrait). In one poem, *Two Birds, A Dialogue,* a big bird [China] rebukes the sparrow [Soviet revisionism] that is obsessed by such unspiritual things as

Potatoes piping hot,
with beef thrown in.

and tells him

Stop your windy nonsense . . .
The whole world is
Turning upside down.

In the other poem, *Chinkiang Mountain,* the one
Mao had referred to so modestly the previous midnight, he wrote exultantly of struggle.

I have long aspired to reach for the clouds . . .

and concluded boldly,

Nothing is impossible,
If you dare to scale the heights.

We were told that the Chairman had taken great interest in our trip, and it became clear to us that he
had meant our midnight meeting as an introduction to
understanding his country and the forces at work in it.
In the days that followed our meeting, I believe that
we saw China almost through his eyes. He not only
dictated what we saw, but he was at the center of all
we saw. Mao was China.

Additionally, in the two days preceding our visit with
the Chairman, we had been shown the quintessential
Maoist sights—a restored portion of the 2,500-mile-
long Great Wall; tht Great Hall of the People, where
not surprisingly we were taken to the Taiwan Room
(which they referred to as "our beloved province"),
and the May 7 Cadre School in the East District of
Peking.

There are several hundred of these revolutionary
schools created by Mao to "reeducate" the bureaucrats
and professionals. In Peking alone, where bureaucrats

abound, there are forty May 7 schools. They exist to remind those potential élitists that in Mao's words, "The masses are the real heroes, while we ourselves are often childish and ignorant." The "students" at these schools are sent to them alone, without their families, to work on the land as the peasants do from six months to two years, and to attend rigorous sessions of ideological criticism and self-criticism.

The school we visited seemed to be in the middle of nowhere, the land around it was flat and winter-barren, a dead tan color. The austere dormitories were like army barracks. We were shown a topographical map of the fields that these educated men and women cultivate. The visit was proof of Mao's determination that no sector of society should advance at the expense of the peasants, who make up eighty percent of the population.

Mao knew the poverty and primitive backwardness of the peasants well. He had lived in rural China for twenty-two years, twelve of them in the caves of Yenan. And in his youth, as an assistant librarian in Peking, he had experienced dire poverty. There was a time when he slept in a room with seven other men, so tightly packed that he had to warn the others when he wanted to turn over. The man who lived intimately with peasants for two decades idealized them. To Mao, every peasant was a hero. In 1959 he wrote:

> I love to look at the multiple waves of rice and
> beans,
> While on every side the heroes return through the
> evening haze.

The most dramatic preparation for our meeting with the Chairman was being taken to look at the poster campaign at Tsinghua University on our very first day in China. A poster campaign at Tsinghua had signaled the beginning of the Cultural Revolution in 1966 when Mao successfully destroyed the existing Communist

Party organization and replaced it with "revolutionary committees" of workers, peasants, and soldiers, all trained to bear arms in the event of Soviet attack, all reminded by Mao that "If no struggle goes on, it means the end of life for any people."

A decade later we were the first Westerners to witness what we were told was a continuation of this revolution. Our visit began with a long discussion with a group of students, peasants, soldiers and a few faculty members. They kept reiterating that the sole purpose of education was to transform the system so that it serves the peasants. Then to reinforce our new awareness that "it is a sin to despise physical labor," the student-peasant-soldier-teachers took us to see the posters. The poster area, merely a narrow alley with a brown, packed-dirt path, is ugly in its bareness. Groups of students, chunky-looking because of the layers of clothes beneath their trousers and Mao jackets, stood silently in front of the posters. The fierce caricatures of the Minister of Education, an alleged élitist, were illuminated by a naked light bulb in the gathering dusk of the late afternoon.

The existence of the sub-surface turmoil in the country became apparent to us very early in our visit, and it gave greater significance to Mao's words on the need for renewed struggle. In our conversations with Chinese officials in Peking, we became aware that there were elements within the Communist hierarchy, especially in the Foreign Ministry, that opposed Mao's relentless attacks against the Soviet Union. On the other hand, Mao's niece, Wang Hai-jung, openly devoted most of her conversation to the evils of the Soviet Union, which led us to believe that in the top echelons of government, Mao, though frail and weakened, was still firmly in control.

Wang Hai-jung's prominence and her anti-Soviet rhetoric reminded us of the harsh Chinese attacks only ten years earlier on American "imperialism." As a worker in the Foreign Ministry in 1966, Wang had been a leader of the Red Guards. During the Cultural Revolution, a conversation between her and Mao in which he told her, "Rebel, when you return to school," was given wide distribution.

Wang Hai-jung gave a luncheon for David and me that featured the famous Peking duck, but I was relieved when the meal was over because her extremely correct attitude toward us was unsettling. It was clear that she was our hostess only because it was her duty as Vice Foreign Minister. We must have reminded her of the hated American capitalists of her schooldays. (I was also relieved that she had waited until after lunch to show us through the hotel kitchen with its rows of greased ducks—all force-fed for four months —in various stages of being roasted.)

Cultural Revolutions are essentially an exercise in redirecting and reigniting hatred in order to unite the people more firmly. Mao used hate as a weapon and rekindled it whenever he felt the threat of revisionism or deviation from his line. It had been a vital force in the Cultural Revolution of 1966, and in 1976 Mao, knowing his death was imminent, was afraid once more that the bureaucracy had become élitist, that revolution was an abstract idea, not a fresh memory. He felt a need for renewed tension, for revitalized Communist fervor. This time the chief villain would be "the grasping hand of Soviet hegemony." And the villain's accomplices would be those in the Foreign Ministry who favored rapproachement with the Soviets.

We watched for signs of the political unheaval that the poster campaign at Tsinghua represented when we visited the four cities on our itinerary outside Peking—Canton, Kweilin, Hangchow and Shanghai. But we saw no evidence that life in these cities had been affected by the "continuing Cultural Revolution." And in the months between our visit and Mao's death, the poster campaign never equaled in intensity the Cultural Revolution of 1966. It seemed to be merely a last gasp by Chairman Mao to reaffirm the need for struggle.

The peasants went on their way to market with their produce as they have for centuries, and on the country roads outside the southern cities of Canton and Kweilin, we saw them toiling under huge loads of sticks and branches, twice as wide and half as tall as they were. The most sensitive political nerve we touched was when we commented on the small pyramid-like mounds that dotted the Kweilin landscape. Our hosts, rather embarrassed, explained that they were peasant graves, disapproved of by Chairman Mao because they were a focus for filial devotion and —perhaps more important—took precious land space. When my parents visited Kweilin six weeks later, we were unable to tell them anything of political importance about the city, which is famous for its beauty. The only valuable information we could offer was to alert them to a certain hardness in the guesthouse accommodations.

We spent a very cold night there in the only guesthouse we stayed in that did not have heat. We had a strange double bed, which I painfully discovered consisted of a wooden platform and a very thin cotton mattress, more mattress pad actually than mattress. After I had undressed for the night, I ran from the bathroom and made a flying leap into bed to get warm —and severely bruised my hip. David solved the rock-hard bed problem by sleeping on the pillows.

Even in the slow-moving, beautiful southern cities, there was always one place where the rigid discipline of revolutionary philosophy engendered by the Cultural Revolution was clear and ever present—the classroom. Repeating Mao's slogan "If the satellite goes up, the Red flag will fall down," the students and teachers emphasized that mass education and revolution were much more important than building satellites or trying to reach the moon. For our part, David and I wondered how much Mao's insistence on a revolutionary mass at the expense of an educated scientific or academic élite would hamper or deny the development of genius among young Chinese.

I remember our arrival at the Shanghai Middle School, timed to coincide with the daily military drill of its fifteen hundred students. Standing on a wooden platform in the bitter cold wind, we watched them drill using wooden sticks for rifles. Later we observed boys and girls at target practice—with real rifles. We received tightly suppressed smiles from the students if they were successful. We toured the factory run by the school, and then visited some of the classrooms—one where students were learning to read English, another where they were making radio parts.

In Chinese classrooms, where the main emphasis is on a new pride in country, ironically there are portraits of four Europeans: Marx, Engels, Lenin and Stalin. Mao viewed Stalin as a great Marxist-Leninist who committed "gross errors without realizing they were errors." Students read publications like *China Youth* that feature heroic descriptions of Mao, such as one of the Chairman at a ship launching, "a fatherly smile on his face, looking at us with saintly eyes that had the warmth of the sun." As a boy, Mao had thought he would be a teacher. Today millions of Chinese children are in Maoist classrooms.

We visited another kind of classroom, where Mao is the focus of life in a highly controlled situation, the commune. Ninety-nine percent of China's peasants, we were told, live in communes. Swedish anthropologist Jan Myrdal's description of a typical commune wedding illustrates how strongly life there is centered on Mao. The bride and groom stand in front of a table laden with sweets, Myrdal reports, and bow low before a portrait of the Chairman. They then answer questions from their family and friends about how they met and how their romance grew. That is the ceremony. The lesson is clear. Mao's philosophy is the only sacrament needed to give meaning to marriage.

A few days before we visited the Tali People's Commune in Canton, David had lightheartedly referred to some of the misconceptions Western observers had of the commune system when it was first established, especially the idea of segregated dormitories, and the eventual breakdown of the family. Because of this, we should have anticipated the kind of "typical house" we would be shown at Tali. It was shared by a husband and wife, their ten-year-old son, six-year-old daughter, their red rooster—and their newly married daughter and her husband. The bride eagerly pointed out every nook and cranny of her bridal bedroom to us —including the colored portrait of Chairman Mao on the bureau, her high-school group photograph, and her wooden hope chest.

We were overwhelmed by the bustling productivity and the atmosphere of self-sufficiency at the Tali People's Commune. The peasants seemed content with Mao's one major concession to their love for the land —private ownership of very small plots. Two "barefoot doctors"—a young man, and a girl about seventeen with thick bangs on her forehead and long braids —were called in from the fields to show us their medical kits, which contained bandages, antiseptics and a few bottles of pills. Their medical knowledge was limited to first aid. In the village the dispensary was stocked with five gallon jugs of snakebite medicine and glass jars of traditional Chinese medicines. An herb garden next to the dispensary provided the ingredients for the medicines. In the commune "hospital" we saw an ingenious incubator—a drawer with an improvised sliding glass top (open just a crack) that held three tiny infants wearing colorful knit caps.

One thing in particular baffled me during our first few days in China, the elaborate seven- and eight-course banquets we were served almost every night— and the inevitable waste of so much food. It made me feel uncomfortably "bourgeois" in that austere society. I was well aware that my hosts shared Mao's view that the workers and peasants "though their hands were soiled and their feet smeared with cow dung . . . were cleaner than the bourgeois and petty bourgeois intellectuals." The Chinese considered us rich, soft capitalists, and we had to accept that role as we traveled in chauffeured limousines and stayed in comfortable guest quarters. But after several banquets, I realized that food is something the Chinese are allowed to enjoy and that our lavish dinners were in themselves a message—"the masses are eating well."

The food was always beautifully arranged. Twice the centerpiece was the mythical bird the phoenix, constructed of multi-colored hors d'oeuvres. Soup was often served in intricately carved gourds, and the desserts were made of glutinous rice in the shapes of goldfish, pandas and other animals, and fruit. With all the rich food, I restricted myself to yogurt and hot, steamed bread for breakfast. I inadvertently endeared myself to our hosts when I told them that I preferred the soft round rolls to the toast the Chinese had thoughtfully prepared for our American-style fried egg breakfasts. I had not realized that steamed bread is what the peasants eat.

It was in the resort city of Hangchow, where the emphasis is on beauty rather than revolution, that I felt Mao's presence most vividly. Our visit to the pagoda-like guesthouse on the west lake in Hangchow was a clear indication that our journey had Mao's official blessing. Or hosts acted as if they were bestowing a great honor. They could hardly suppress their own excitement.

It was a pale-green house with a red-tiled roof in a setting of fairy-tale beauty on the edge of the lake. Graceful, curving branches were mirrored in still pools. Mist rising from the pools bathed the leaves and branches in a heavy dew. The only sounds were peaceful ones—geese honking on the lake and the gentle lapping of the water against the shore.

A sentry box surveyed the entrance and People's

Liberation Army soldiers patrolled the grounds. At one point I opened a door onto the terrace and was startled to come face to face with two of the guards.

In the living room, Ambassador Huang-chen showed me the piano my father had played during his visit in 1972, and a movie screen concealed behind a beautiful scroll. Our hosts were avidly curious and whispered among themselves as we looked at the two main bedrooms and their large bathrooms. The rooms were nicely but not extravagantly furnished. There was no art on the walls. The warmth in the rooms came from the silk bed covers and rugs in the same color as the spreads. I was slightly embarrassed when the Chinese spent several minutes looking at the luxurious bathrooms, with their toilet seats completely covered in fuzzy cotton.

At the end of the tour, as we sat in the living room eating tangerines, I had the feeling that our Chinese friends did not want to leave. It was not until I learned that this house was the favorite retreat of Chairman Mao and Premier Chou En-lai that I understood the eagerness and reverence with which they absorbed every detail.

Our tour of China ended in Shanghai, a crowded, bleak city of 11,000,000, its streets filled with relentlessly purposeful people going to and from work. It was a startling contrast to Hangchow. In Shanghai there were constant reminders of Mao's demand that his people live selflessly for the state.

In a hospital so cold that the patients wore their coats in bed, the Chinese proudly described their pioneering work in restoring severed hands and feet, toes and fingers. One girl, whose fingers and half her palm had been cut off in an accident and sewn back on by the doctors, showed us how she could move her fingers ever so slightly twelve months after the accident. She was introduced to us as "an educated youth who went to the countryside to work with the peasants." Her tragic accident reminded David and me of the hazards that educated Chinese face when forced to do unfamiliar manual work.

A beautiful ballerina, a member of the district Revolutionary Committee, was one of our hosts at a dinner in Shanghai. Feathery wisps of hair fell across her forehead, the rest was pulled back in a sophisticated knot at the nape of her neck. She sat with her ankles gracefully crossed, and in a quiet, shy voice told us how she had spent the previous year working in the fields during the day and dancing on the ground at night for the peasants. There was no point in asking her how a year away from the discipline and structured life of a ballet troupe had affected her ability to perfect her art. It is not easy in China to question the idea of self-sacrifice.

Mao believed that the goal of art should be to enable the masses to understand what they see or hear; propaganda was essential. It was a cultural shock to see Chinese ballet and discover that the most difficult artistic feat the *Red Detachment of Women* dancers performed was to aim their rifles at the air above the heads of the audience as they did splits. Beautiful art work is still to be found in China, but most of it is for the export trade. For example, we saw one large exquisite ivory sculpture—priced at no less than 50,000 American dollars! The overwhelming emphasis in art is on revolutionary propaganda. The ceramics factory we visited in Canton was mass-producing black soldiers with clenched fists and upraised rifles for export to Africa.

It was impossible for us to forget the bitterness between the West and China. No day went by without a short lecture detailing Chinese grievances against the "running dogs of imperialism" and the "gangsters who would reverse the great gains of proletarian socialism." But the lectures were delivered with a kind of benign or diffident detachment, which seemed to indicate that either the words meant less now or that David and I had been set apart for the time being from the "hated gang of revanchist conspirators" because of our New Year's Eve visit with the Chairman. Except for these moments our trip was relatively carefree—until we arrived in Shanghai.

Three of the five Chinese who traveled with us had been born in Shanghai and were old enough to remember the era of the foreign economic and trade concessions and the presence of Western navies. Anti-Western feeling still runs deep in Shanghai. The local organization is radical. It was from Shanghai that Mao launched the Cultural Revolution.

When we arrived in the city, an undefined mood of uneasiness came over our official group. The interpreter, Mr. Ni, became "ill" and uncommunicative; the others became somber. Every remnant of the Western imperialist presence was pointed out to us as we drove through the city.

"On your left, we have the Cultural Hall, which, as you may recall reading, was once a British brothel."

There were no smiles. The spontaneity and sense of discovery we had shared had suddenly dissipated. For our Shanghai-born companions, the memories were strong and the associations bitter.

We spent the first night there at a banquet given by the Shanghai Revolutionary Committee. Our host, the Vice Chairman, was thoughtful, intellectual, and conversed freely regarding trends abroad. Unlike other Chinese we met, he seemed to take special pride in his appearance. His Mao suit fit well. His hair was skillfully trimmed. At his insistence, we tried to guess his age and were surprised to learn that he was over forty.

We played word games during dinner and described the current film rage at home, *Jaws*. Our host told us that "the people of Shanghai would not allow such a silly film. They would tear down the theater!" The conversation was pleasant and easy until Ambassador Huang-chen's wife interrupted with a seemingly random observation, "I read today in *The People's Daily* that the life expectancy in Shanghai is now seventy-three years."

Everyone nodded vigorous approval and our host leaned over to tell us, "Before liberation, people died on the streets. The life expectancy was only forty-nine years." And everyone nodded again.

The Vice Chairman pressed on. "I remember when I was a boy, about sixteen, I used to read an American publication called *Miller's Review*."

He paused. Were we supposed to have heard of *Miller's Review?* I glanced at Ni, our interpreter—Shanghai-born, bald, unkempt, a dedicated revolutionary with a genuine love for children. His gentle demeanor had hardened. He was perspiring and, quite uncharacteristically, staring directly at us as he translated. It was as though he, too, recalled reading *Miller's Review* as a boy and marveled that our faces did not register recognition when we heard the name.

"And I remember a particular story in *Miller's Review*." The words had now become Ni's. "There was a little item one day at the bottom of the back page. And do you know what it said?"

The Vice Chairman gazed off into space, but Ni's eyes were fixed on our faces as he translated.

"There was a wind in the northeast section of town last night. And in the morning, eight hundred bodies were picked up."

Ni stared at us, then shook his head.

Silence.

After this the conversation limped along until we left, tired and disturbed. The spell had been broken. Now we remembered who we were and they remembered who we were and what we stood for. It was Westerners who had callously dismissed eight hundred Chinese deaths with a small item on the back page of *Miller's Review*.

Mao had changed much in his country, but not the memories. Suddenly I saw his intense struggle against a legacy of thousands of years of grinding poverty more clearly and understood his constant exhortations that the peasants, once discounted and powerless, must be unified behind his cause.

One wonders if Mao exalted the masses and proclaimed the revolutionary power of the human will because few other options were open to him. During China's struggle for survival as a nation since 1949, there have been times when there were not enough guns, but there have always been enough men. In Korea in 1951, only the first line of men had guns. Wave after wave of young soldiers who followed behind picked up the guns of fallen comrades. When the Soviet Union abruptly cut off their aid in 1960, there was not enough gasoline, but there were always enough men to bear burdens, pull carts and walk or bicycle to work. In 1976, Mao, his country still lagging behind the West in developing nuclear capability, proclaimed that wars were not decided by nuclear weapons but by the courage and perseverance of the men who fight.

Mao's philosophy was a response to the economic realities of material poverty and an almost unlimited supply of manpower, but it was more than just a response; it was a design, a religion for daily life which applied to men whether or not they were impoverished. He believed "the strongest fort is our will." He believed in the capability of men to struggle and to succeed. He was a philosopher who never stopped trying to reform man, even though the realist in him told him it was impossible.

Mao Tse-tung wiped out almost all vestiges of Imperial China. His battle was against a deeply ingrained tradition of harmony and order. His victory represented a staggering reversal, destroying two thousand years of loyalty to Confucian culture and substituting it with the harsh concept of unending struggle.

When we met with Mao, he had been tempered by illness and by age. His philosophical self-confidence must have been shaken by the bitterness of the breach with the Soviet Union, which claims the same philosophy of revolution and brotherhood. Yet, I suspect that the words he wrote in 1949 to a friend of his revolutionary days in Canton are words he would have reaffirmed even as he faced death. "Do not let too much sorrow break your heart. Keep the whole world always in your far-sighted eyes."

In China, it was often difficult for David and me to follow that advice and keep the whole world in our eyes. Morning after morning we were mesmerized by the sight of thousands on foot, dressed alike, on their way to work, with the realization that in cities we never saw there were millions more, all delicately balanced on the edge of poverty. It was difficult not to be overwhelmed by the zeal with which they approached their bleak existence.

There were times when it seemed as if our long days in China would never come to an end, even though we were tightly scheduled with few free moments. It was inconceivable that we would soon return to the world of "you deserve a break today."

The weight and intensity of political thought was so great that one expected the slightest crack would destroy the whole structure. Yet on January 9, as we prepared to fly back home, China suffered a major blow that appeared to us to cause only a ripple of reaction—the death of Premier Chou En-lai.*

We received the news from an American journalist thousands of miles away in New York. His telephone call wakened us in Shanghai at seven-thirty, but the jolting news was not confirmed until Ambassador Huang-chen's aide came to our bedroom an hour later to advise us formally of the Premier's death. It was the morning of my father's sixty-third birthday.

---

* Soon after our arrival, we had been told that Premier Chou En-lai was too ill for us to deliver my father's letter to him personally, so I had given it to the Foreign Minister to transmit to the Premier.

I was surprised to hear the blare of martial music over loudspeakers, the same music we had heard the morning before. The hotel staff brought in a beautiful vanilla birthday cake with white and brown frosting, presumably for David and me to have with breakfast. And in a silk-covered box was an even larger cake, decorated with the Chinese characters for "Happy Birthday, Mr. Nixon," to take home to my father.

There was sorrow on the faces of the Chinese we saw that morning at the hotel, but everything else was the same. Despite the blow of Chou's death—and there would be emotional mass demonstrations after his funeral—our hosts made it clear to us that in the end, it is the masses who count, not the leaders. Chou's death would not change the course of history. Unspoken, but unavoidable, was the message that Mao's death would not change things either. In a sense, Mao had already passed into history. He was godlike, remote. China's strength would not be diminished by her god's physical demise.

I feel sure that in his declining years, Mao was aware of his place in history. He had always felt he was a man of destiny. As early as 1919, he had prophesied that "one day the reform of the Chinese people will be more profound than that of any other people . . . an age of glory and splendor lies before us." His words were always carefully chosen as if he were speaking for history. Even in those dark days of retreat in Yenan in the Thirties, when he was interviewed by Edgar Snow, he used to insist that after Snow had written the interview in English it be translated back into Chinese. Then Mao would make corrections before giving his approval.

But the man who was realistic enough to see China's shortcomings must have been realistic enough to see his own. He must have anticipated that his successors might come to find fault with him, just as Stalin's found fault with him, and Khrushchev's with him. Mao's legacy, while great, is flawed. He attained goals that had once seemed visionary, but at a fearful price. His life, perhaps above all others, gave rise to the violent and increasingly revolutionary demands of the world's poor. He advanced a global struggle that has and will continue to bring enormous dislocation and change—and death. From his early days in Canton through the years in Yenan and finally in Peking, death and violence were inextricably entwined with revolutionary idealism. Whatever history decides, Mao's life will stand as a testament to the power of the human will.

When we met with the Chairman in the middle of the night, we had an impression of a man restless in solitude. He was drawn and spent. Yet each time we started to leave, he ordered us to stay—almost as if he were clinging to visitors who possessed opportunities he may have wished were his again.

His painful vulnerability reminded David and me of the hours we had spent with President Eisenhower before he died. Sitting at his bedside, at Walter Reed Army Hospital, we had been deeply conscious of our youth, of the opportunities ahead, and of the roads we had yet to travel. It was also a reminder of how carelessly we live—and how much can be lost and wasted by living life casually.

We experienced the same emotions that New Year's Eve. When we finally got up to leave and the Foreign Minister led us to the door of the study, Mao had walked with us. We were told later that he had not made such a gesture for over two years. I felt sad when I shook his hand in farewell.

"You people are young," he said. "Come back to China. In ten years she will be great." He no longer smiled. The two nurses stood by his side supporting him. He waved twice as we disappeared into the darkness of the next room. I looked back for a moment. My last glimpse was of a weary old man, turning, attempting words with his nurses, then gently being led away to be alone again.

I like to think that Mao may have been tempted to give us advice, as the old advise the young, when we said good-bye. If he had, I believe it would have been those words that he repeated over and over for so many years, that were the very rhythm of his life:

"Ten thousand years is too long. Seize the day! Seize the hour!"

Mam e
Doud
Eisenhower

"Don't give them any of that prissy stuff. Give them a big wave. Really say hello."

MAMIE DOUD EISENHOWER has star quality. To a little girl, she outshone the President. I remember my first visit to the family quarters of the White House as if it were yesterday, not because I saw the intriguing upstairs home of the President, nor because of the historical significance of the day, but because of Mamie. I liked her because she laughed so much. It was on January 20, 1957. Because the 20th fell on a Sunday that inaugural year, there was a private inaugural ceremony at the White House in the morning so that Chief Justice Earl Warren could swear in President Eisenhower and my father for their second terms.

I had met Mrs. Eisenhower before, but only for the briefest of white-gloved handshakes. As my parents and my sister and I drove down Pennsylvania Avenue for the ceremony, I was excited because I was going to see where the President lived. I remember being surprised that we used an elevator to go from the ground floor to the East Room one floor above. To my mind, the visit was all too short. The swearing-in ceremony took less than fifteen minutes. Refreshments were served afterward but my Coke was gone in minutes, and we all just stood in the big room—which was empty except for a piano and several gold chairs—and talked. There was no opportunity to see anything —no bedrooms, no kitchen, no pets.

When we were escorted to the elevator to leave, I started to cry. Mamie and my mother bent down, very concerned. Through my tears I explained I wanted to play in the White House.

Mamie smiled and invited Tricia and me to stay for lunch with David and his sisters, Anne, who was seven, and Susie, five years old. There was creamed chicken mounded into a tall ring of white rice. I had never seen rice that "stood up" by itself before, and I was very impressed. We had peas and, to my dismay, tall glasses of milk. I hated milk. Afterward, David took us outdoors to play. We chased each other around the paved path that circles the magnolia tree planted by Andrew Jackson. All of a sudden, Mrs. Eisenhower appeared at the double-door entrance to the White House. "David, David! Come here!" she commanded.

Her grandchildren froze in their tracks. David was scolded for bringing his sisters and guests outside without coats. I do not remember much more about the visit except that I fell in love with Anne and Susie's four-story doll house and spent the rest of the visit playing dolls in the third-floor playroom.

In 1973, sixteen years after that visit upstairs at the White House, I drove down Pennsylvania Avenue again to another inaugural. Ike was no longer with us, but Mamie was in the car with me on the way to witness my father being sworn in to his second term as President. David was in the Navy then, on duty in the Mediterranean with the Sixth Fleet, and Mamie told everyone, "I'm playing David." The same self-assured, utterly natural quality that had impressed me as an eight-year-old was still very much in evidence.

During the ride down Pennsylvania Avenue to the Capitol, I gave an occasional timid wave to the crowds lining the streets. "Don't give them any of that prissy stuff," Mamie said. "Give them a big wave. Really say hello." And with that she stretched her arm out the window and, holding her hand high, waved it proudly like a flag.

The sight of Mamie waving must have been a flashback to the Eisenhower Administration for many people along the route. I could not help but feel disappointed that all they saw that day was her cheery smile and her big wave, little more than she had revealed during her eight years as First Lady. Mamie had seen her role as one of emotional support for her husband—and nothing else. That star quality she possessed could have catapulted her into a position of constant public attention and adulation. The country could have come to understand the strength, the endurance and the utter charm of Mamie Eisenhower. But public recognition could not have mattered less to her. She had no interest in promoting herself.

Up until the time of President Eisenhower's third heart attack in March, 1968, I had known Mamie only as a light-hearted, fun-loving future grandmother-in-law and a woman, as one of her friends put it, "with a whim of iron." My image of her was little more than "Smiles, Bangs and Jewelry," the subtitle of one of her biographies.

Tragedy showed me another side of her character and I came to have a great respect and admiration for Mamie as well as love. She had been tested many times. There had been the death of her firstborn son at age four and the uprooting strain of nearly three dozen moves before she and Ike finally retired to Gettysburg. There had been the long war years when Mamie was home alone with her Army wife's knowledge of the dangers her husband faced, along with rumors of romance. And later the anxiety of having her only son in the combat zone during the Korean War. But the supreme test must have been the eleven months at Walter Reed Army Hospital in Washington, D.C., when she lived in a small room just a few yards down the hospital corridor from her husband, the months of Ike's dying. Ike never saw her waver or weaken. Even the family rarely did. There were only a few times when her eyes, blue and round as a porcelain doll's, filled with tears. But she never cried in self-pity. Her tears came from the sorrowful knowledge of how little she could do for Ike, from the realization that he was ultimately alone in his suffering, alone in his dying.

It was a sadness we all shared. In my diary I wrote on June 16, the day after President Eisenhower suffered his fourth heart attack, "David is heartbroken because he pictures his grandfather as a maverick who would like to ride off into the hills and die with his boots on." That attack marked the beginning of the period when Mamie and her family had to stand by and watch as Ike, for the first time in his life, found that he no longer could control his destiny.

He fought his illness with courage, as he had fought all his battles. In August, he decided he was strong enough to address the Republican National Convention by television. His decision proved to be a fateful one. Mamie knew, even before the television cameras were set up in the living room of Ward Eight at Walter Reed, how much effort, how much emotion this speech represented for Ike. The next morning he suffered his fifth myocardial infraction. He never left his bed again. And Mamie knew that the strain of the speech was the main cause of this fifth heart attack.

Mamie had not tried to stop Ike from making the speech, nor did she resent this final devotion to duty. Ike's credo was her credo—duty, honor, country. Not that she did not put up a fight upon occasion for him to consider his own well-being and that of his family first. But that August, Mamie gave the impression in her every act and look that if Ike had to suffer one more cruel, breath-stopping heart attack, she was reconciled. Reconciled because Ike also knew the cost of this final act of duty—and accepted it as part of his service to the political party he had helped strengthen and in the cause of the country he loved.

From that day on, her life revolved almost completely around her husband. There were weeks and weeks when she never left the hospital. One exception was a surprise birthday party we gave for my mother. Mamie told us she could not accept the invitation until the last moment. It would have to depend on what kind of day Ike was having. She did come, but as soon as the cake was cut she left. "My beau is waiting up to hear all about the party," she explained to my mother. She told me later that Ike was awake when she arrived back at the hospital. She stood near his pillow in the darkened room and described the toasts, the piano playing, and how much he had been missed.

She guarded his energy jealously, allowing one old friend a ten-minute visit, another a stingy five minutes. I was touched by the way she denied herself the pleasure of seeing Ike with his grandchildren. She believed that more than two visitors at a time was too draining, so David and I would visit while she watched the clock in her room. When our time was up, the nurse would appear. "On Mrs. Eisenhower's orders, the time is up," she would say. Ike often insisted we stay longer, but within minutes, Mamie would come bouncing into the room, her wide, petticoated skirt swinging, and we would be cheerfully, but firmly, hustled out. Playing warden with people Ike wanted to see must have been a painful role for her at times. Another difficult task was censoring news that would excite or upset Ike. He was not told about the rioting at Columbia University in the spring of 1968 until the disturbances had quieted down, nor was he allowed to watch the annual Army-Navy game on television. Mamie filtered the progress of the game to the frustrated onetime Army football coach.

Mamie's efforts—strongly encouraged by the doctors—to regulate Ike's visiting hours resulted in what must rank as one of the classic Secret Service radio communications. David and I, who were both in college at that time, visited his grandfather as often as we could. One evening our trip from Northampton, Massachusetts, took longer than usual. We were in a Secret Service car, silent because we did not want to share our conversation with the agents, and they were as constrained as we were. Suddenly the silence was broken by a message crackling over the intercom. "Springtime advises you hurry. It is past Scoreboard's bedtime." Sunbonnet (Julie) and Sahara (David) had a good laugh, as did the agents in the front seat.

Mamie lived in a tiny sitting room and bedroom (complete with high hospital bed) just down the hall from Ike's suite. Apart from her hot pink telephone and the tins of cookies and boxes of fudge from friends, the room was surprisingly empty of personal belongings for a woman who loved to surround herself with knickknacks and family photographs. Perhaps her reluctance to bring personal objects to the hospital, like the tiny Coke bottle that was really a lighter and the miniature megaphone that contained a picture of Mamie, which had been on her bedside table as long as her grandchildren could remember, was an unconscious refusal to accept the gravity of Ike's illness. She was not blind to the deterioration in his condition—I remember the summer day when she was sad because "Ike will never be able to play golf again"—but she never gave up hope that one day the doctor would come in and tell her that Ike would be going home next week.

Mamie disliked closed doors and the sense of being shut in, so her door onto the hall was always slightly ajar, making it impossible to forget for one minute that she was in a hospital. There was a constant traffic of doctors and nurses up and down the stark white hall with its harsh fluorescent lighting. The windows of her rooms were sealed. The changing seasons outside did not touch those within. There were no scents of autumn leaves or the fresh smell after a rain.

She used to spend hours sewing facecloths together with long, looping stitches of thick yarn and stuffing them with foam to make pillows for her friends. And she politicked. She kept a bowl of Nixon buttons on the coffee table. I did not realize the extent to which she pushed my father's candidacy until one afternoon shortly before he won the Republican nomination, I met two soon-to-be relatives—Milton Eisenhower's daughter and son-in-law—who were visiting Ike. They were wearing Nixon buttons. I was elated and surprised since I knew the General's brother was not an avid Nixon campaigner. I learned much later that Mamie passed out buttons to everyone—visitors and doctors alike. Most found her "gift" difficult to refuse.

Despite the fact that she was in essence camping out at Walter Reed, she managed to create a happy atmosphere on special occasions. I remember particularly our Thanksgiving at the hospital in 1968. My parents, Tricia and I joined David and his family in the main dining room of Ward Eight. We had a traditional turkey dinner, the same Army fare being served throughout the hospital.

With the precision of an Army drill instructor, Mamie arranged for members of each family to share a course of the meal with Ike in his bedroom. Susie Eisenhower and Tricia had juice with him, David and I had fruit cup, and so on, until the pumpkin pie with my mother and David's mother. Mamie, at the head of the table, daintily but firmly orchestrated the entrances and exits of everyone from my father to David's twelve-year-old sister, Mary. As we went in and out of Ike's room that day, we had to pass the rows of monitors, a vivid reminder that this might be his last Thanksgiving.

Neither Ike nor Mamie lost their courage—or their humor. David and I visited him a month before the election. He was lying flat in bed, his head just slightly raised. He was so thin and wasted under the Army-issue sheet. The blueness of his eyes was startling in his dead-white face. When I kissed his cheek, I was surprised by the trace of beard stubble. Somehow I felt the lifeless skin could not produce a beard. As soon as we said hello, Ike gave us a huge grin and whipped open his hospital smock, exposing his Nixon "buttons." He had stuck Nixon decals on the electrodes attached to his chest.

When the morning came that the doctors told Mamie
that her husband would not live through the day, she
sat stoically in her chair by the window in the sitting
room, a small figure, crumpled and silent, but a figure
of dignity. Her sister, "Mike" Moore, Barbara Eisenhower and I did not try to offer words of comfort.
There were none. Mamie, who had remained at Ike's
side through so many months, had no interest in the
deathwatch. Only at the very end, accompanied by
John Eisenhower and David, did she slip into Ike's
bedroom for one last look, to touch his hand one last
time.

The thought of "what Ike would expect" sustained
Mamie through the four days of state funeral ceremonies. She met privately with many of the world leaders
who came to Washington to pay final tribute to President Eisenhower, including Charles de Gaulle. The
family had been excited when they learned he was
coming to see her, but Mamie, who had never been
awed by the famous or the powerful, simply welcomed
him as the old acquaintance that he was. De Gaulle
had tears in his eyes when he bent over to kiss the
hand of the frail woman who would carry on General
Eisenhower's name and honor. Mamie was seated on
a small sofa and she patted the cushion next to her in
a motion for "Mr. Presidente" to join her. He did not
blink an eye at the Spanish pronunciation of his title.
Mamie sat calmly with the wartime leader of free
Frenchmen everywhere. She vulnerable, and yet full
of strength in her self-composure. He a hulking, tall
figure, but gray—gray skin and hair, a gray film over
his eyes, stooped and older now in his sorrow at Ike's
death.

President Eisenhower's body was borne by train
across the heartland of his country to his boyhood
home, Abilene, Kansas. Mamie lay in her bed by the
window and all through the night, as Ike would have
wished, she waved to the little clusters of people standing beside the tracks. Before reaching Abilene, she

ordered the train halted and a flag placed on the car bearing Ike so that his countrymen might know where he lay.

He was buried on David's twenty-first birthday. That night as the train returned to Washington, Mamie arranged for a birthday cake. She stood in the doorway of the dining car, her eyes glistening, holding on to her sister's arm as the train lurched, and sang "Happy Birthday" to Ike's namesake. The ceremonies were over. Mamie Eisenhower had to pick up the strands of her life. She had to go on.

As the wife of a great man, fame had touched Mamie Doud Eisenhower as well as her husband. Yet she remained remarkably unchanged. She was unconcerned with her public image, indifferent while at the eye of the storm of press attention, and indifferent now in retrospect. She does not pretend to be anything more than what one sees on the surface—a pleasantly rounded grandmother with a perky fringe of bangs beneath a flowered hat. A grandmother and an attractive woman with great feminine charm. Most of all, she was the woman behind the man, the woman who proudly proclaimed, "Ike was my career."

Mamie and Ike were plain folks, as common as cherry pie. Mamie mirrored to an incredible degree the moods and mores of the Fifties. Happily, the emphasis on the old-fashioned virtues of wife and homemaker fit Mamie's natural lifestyle, because if one thing is certain about Mamie Doud Eisenhower, it is that she would not have changed herself to fit the Fifties.

She was nineteen when she first met Dwight Eisenhower, attracted to him because, as she told her grandson, she was sick of being courted by "all those lounge lizards with patent leather hair." Ike was different. "He was a bruiser," Mamie recalls proudly, well-built and handsome. Most intriguing of all to the flirtatious Mamie Doud, he had a reputation as a woman hater. She changed that. During their courtship, Ike often found himself sitting on the front porch with Papa

Doud—waiting for Mamie to return from a date with another young man. She was irresistible. The newly commissioned Second Lieutenant inscribed his West Point photograph "to the dearest and sweetest girl in the world." It was a traditional inscription considering the quality that most caught his fancy—her sauciness. Mamie was charmingly saucy—and, as he learned later, as strong-willed as he.

She knew exactly what she liked and did not like right down to the colors she would wear and those she would not wear. The woman with the china-blue eyes rarely wore blue blouses because it did "terrible things" to her skin. Ike was to discover that often there was no logic behind her likes and dislikes or her reasoning. Some things in their marriage, including their bridge partnership, could not survive Mamie's carefree, "my way" attitude.

A typical scene at the bridge table:

Mamie bids.

Ike (making a valiant effort not to yell): "Why did you make that play?"

Mamie (with a pouting underlip and a shrug of her shoulders): "Oh, I don't know. Just 'cause I wanted to."

Ike throws his hand down, leaves bridge table in disgust, his face a flame color.

End of scene.

When Mamie talks about learning to live with Ike, she frequently contradicts herself. She never fails to remind me when I visit her in Gettysburg that, "There can be only one star in the heaven, sugar, and there is only one way to live with an Eisenhower. Let him have his own way." At other times, she pertly boasts, "Ike never told me what I should do, because he knew I'd go right out and do the exact opposite." Throughout their fifty-two years together, it was a sometimes tempestuous relationship which was least subject to strain when they had public roles to fulfill.

The responsibility of being on view disciplined their lives and drew them together.

Mamie took a long time to grow up. "I was rotten spoiled," she says cheerfully. Her parents pampered her and Mamie adored them. She was unusually close to her mother. Fortunately, Ike and Mrs. Doud (he called her Min) became good friends at the very beginning. Min lived with them in the White House for months at a time, until 1958 when ill health forced her to return to her home in Denver.

Mamie's deep love for her family was to be a bond between my grandmother-in-law and me. I have never felt closer to her than on the evening of my parents' departure for their first Presidential trip to Asia in 1969. It was a sultry, rainy night. After we watched them board Air Force One, Mamie, Tricia, David and I sat in one of the limousines to watch the takeoff out of the rain. Tears welled up in my eyes. I could not repress the thought that something awful might happen—a crash, an assassin's bullet. It was one of those moments when you realize how uncertain life is and how precious parents are. Suddenly, I felt Mamie's hand, so small and fragile. She closed her fingers over mine. All she said was, "I understand." And I knew that she did.

When Mamie was married in 1916, it marked a wrenching break with her three sisters and her parents, to whom she had confided every emotion. She had to adjust to a husband who rarely verbalized affection and who had no use for small talk. A slap on the back between the shoulder blades or a pinch was Ike's way of saying "I love you." His career as an Army man made Mamie's adjustment to marriage even more difficult. Before her wedding she had never spent a night alone. She knew little of the world beyond the comfortably well-to-do Doud household.

In making a home out of the two rooms that had been Ike's bachelor quarters at Fort Sam Houston outside San Antonio, Mamie added her own touches of elegance. With a twinkle she described to me how she rented a piano for five dollars a month and then to make room for it, she stashed all the "inessentials," like Ike's field equipment and revolver, behind it. But decorating was like playing house. What was harder for a sheltered girl was adjusting to the realities of Army existence—the abrupt orders to move, the hardship posts, the separations.

One month after the wedding, Ike had to leave on maneuvers. Mamie protested. Ike put his arms around her. "Mamie, there's one thing you must understand," he said. "My country comes first and always will. You come second." Mamie was nineteen then and it took her many years to learn to live with that statement. I suspect that it was not until Ike was President of the United States that she came to fully accept second place.

Ike had told Mamie that his country came first, but he might have phrased it differently after the birth of his son. He was on field assignment at Fort Oglethorpe in Georgia when Doud Dwight was born in San Antonio. Mamie makes the arrival of her baby sound like a slapstick comedy, but it must have been a frightening experience. A few days after Ike had left for Georgia, near eleven o'clock at night Mamie decided to mail a letter to him. Although barely able to drive—Ike had given her a few crash lessons before he departed—she took the car. When she came back she had a stomachache. She thought it was due to the nervous tension of driving alone in the dark. So she ate an orange in the hope that would make her feel better. Mamie told me, "Mama [Min Doud was staying with her] took an awful long time to explain about the stomachache!" Mamie spent most of that endless night sitting up in a rocking chair. In the morning, Mama Doud somehow arranged to have Mamie taken to the post infirmary—lying down in the back of a rickety, horse-drawn cart. To the surprise of the doctor, who had sent Mrs. Doud out for breakfast, the baby was born a half hour later.

Mamie and Ike loved Icky, as they called their baby, more than anything else in the world. They had never been closer than during Mamie's pregnancy. Ike had watched Mamie, who had no knowledge of sewing (it was he who had let out many of her dresses during pregnancy), lovingly stitch a long white christening gown. When Icky died four years later from scarlet fever, a deep sorrow separated his parents. Mamie had always expressed her emotions—every complaint, every thought, petty or important. Ike, to his dying day, found it difficult to express his feelings. Now they were tragically alone in their reactions to the death of their son. She grieved openly, he silently.

The depth of Ike's despair comes through even in his restrained account of Icky's death in his book *At Ease*. It was "the greatest disappointment and disaster in my life, the one I have never been able to forget completely," he wrote. Icky was buried in the Doud family plot in Denver, but when Ike made plans for his own burial in Abilene, he arranged for Icky to be re-interred there. On March 31, 1969, Mamie watched Ike's casket placed under a honey-colored marble slab. Another slab, as yet blank, lay beside him. At his feet was a tiny marble marker for Doud Dwight Eisenhower. Icky could not be left alone in Denver. To his parents, he was forever a child in need of nurture.

Half a century later, Mamie was still unwilling to say much about how Icky's death changed her relationship with Ike. The pain is too deep. But there is no doubt that the loss of their beloved son closed a chapter in the marriage. It could never again be unblemished first love. Ike was no longer an untried idealist, Mamie no longer a blithely romantic spirit. Now they regarded each other with open eyes.

When Mamie talks about her marriage, she paints no rosy, unrealistic pictures. "There were a lot of times when Ike broke my heart," she told me one rainy afternoon in Gettysburg. She was propped up in bed, where she spends more and more of her time, surrounded by books, photographs, boxes of candy, letter paper. "I wouldn't have stood it for a minute if I didn't respect him. It was the kind of thing where I respected him so much, I didn't want to do anything to disappoint him." Her face was uncharacteristically sad as if she were looking back on the times when she had disappointed him.

Mamie blames herself for many of the strains on their marriage, and says she would like to be able to go back and do some things differently.

John Eisenhower was born one year after his brother died and came to be the greatest source of happiness in their lives. Ike always wanted John to have brothers and sisters and Mamie now realizes it was hard for their son to be an only child. She explained, "I always felt there was plenty of time to have another child," but the years of constant uprooting rushed by. Ike was so convinced of the desirability of large families that later on he persistently—and insistently—tried to persuade his son and daughter-in-law to have a fifth child. Despite a healthy "bribe," they decided four children were sufficient.

More than anything else Mamie regrets that she gave in to the temptation to go "home" to Denver so often. The only times I ever felt Mamie was meddling in my marriage were when she strongly advised that I join David whenever we were separated by school or the Navy or campaign travels. I never resented this "meddling," because I sensed the reason for her urgency. Mamie had learned that there were always plenty of women waiting to bat their eyes at handsome young officers.

It is easier to understand her frequent, prolonged absences when one considers some of the homes she and Ike shared. In Laurel, Maryland, in 1919, the only place they could find was a rooming house several miles from the post, where the electricity was turned off at eight in the morning and did not go back on until after dark. Night after night, Mamie sat in their gloomy room with a two-and-a-half-year-old toddler waiting for Ike to come home—and the lights to go on. The only bathroom was down the hall. They ate at a boarding house around the corner. She lasted ten days there. Mamie's voice was anguished when she described the scene when she fled back home to Denver half a century before. "Ike begged me to stay," she said, "but I told him, 'Ike, I can't live my life this way.' " And Mamie took Icky and went to Denver.

In 1923, when she was pregnant with John, she sailed with Ike on a troop transport to his new station in Panama. Because of her severe claustrophobia, she refused to sleep on the bunks one on top of the other with only twelve inches between. Instead, she spent the nights on a short couch—so short she had to sleep in a jackknife position—for the week-and-a-half trip. And the Army post in Panama was not much improvement over the troop ship. It was all the nightmares of a gently-bred girl come true. Their first night in Panama, a rat gnawed at their bedroom door until daybreak. The cockroaches were "the size of mice." The legs of their bed stood in pans of kerosene to fend off the bedbugs. And, worst of all, a bat swooped down at them as they were getting ready for bed that first night. Mamie told me proudly how her hero, Ike, stood on the bed, unsheathed his sword and swung wildly at the bat, "just like Douglas Fairbanks." She laughed when she described that night, but at the time it was not at all amusing. In fact, life in Panama was as alien to Mamie as life on Mars. Within a few months, she was back in Denver again, where John Eisenhower was born.

Mamie's frequent retreats to the Doud home, whether because of inadequate housing or one of Ike's long absences on maneuvers or other duty, created tension in her marriage. She leaned on her parents for emotional support as she had before her marriage, and now they came to lean on her. When her older sister Eleanor died in 1918, Mamie spent six months with her family. She had been married only two years at the time. It was pleasant being home where family and servants cared for her and her child. It was impossible not to contrast how well her family provided for her, how comfortable she was at home, with the life Ike could give her on an Army salary, moving from base to base.

And yet the luxuries from Ike, like Mamie's silver tea service, were far sweeter, because they were so dearly bought, and a testament of his deep love. When the Eisenhowers lived in Washington from 1927 until 1935, Ike used to save as much of his five-dollars-a-week lunch and transportation allowance as he could —often walking several miles home from the old State-War-Navy Building. With this money and with his poker winnings, he bought Mamie the tea service —precious piece by precious piece.

Each time Mamie and Ike were reunited after a separation, she had to accept his decisions for their life, a change from the enforced independence she had had to assume when he went away, a change from the role of daughter that she enjoyed at home with her parents to that of a wife. Abruptly she was expected to fulfill Ike's needs in a wife—to be a woman, not a girl; someone to place on a pedestal, not a cute, volatile child to be coddled; someone to provide a haven from the pressures of his job. Mamie often said that Ike never brought his problems home with him and she never offered advice. "He didn't need that kind of help from me." The kind of help he needed was something Mamie seemed to have to learn how to give all over again after every retreat of hers to the family bosom. It is to the credit of both Mamie and Ike, and an example of their mutual respect, that despite the unusual strains created by Army life and their subsequent strong disagreements their son could write in his memoirs, "They never quarreled in front of me."

The Army Mamie knew was one of hardship for married couples, and yet she came to like this world that was so different from her own. When I asked her why, she told me of taking Icky's body to Denver for burial a few days before Christmas. Upon her return home to Camp Meade, Maryland, the men and women at the post had taken down their Christmas tree, put the red tricycle and other Christmas presents out of sight, packed up his clothes and toys. Mamie was to find comfort and support many times in the tightly knit Army family.

And so she endured thirty-four moves. Her furniture often did not fare as well as she. During the transit from Washington to the Philippines in 1937, all her china was smashed and not a single chair came through undamaged. Ike was home for only one of those moves. At Fort Lewis, Washington, in 1939, he tried to help, but, as Mamie told me, he only "muddied the water." He randomly shoved boxes and unprotected furniture into the van. Did Mamie protest his "help"? "Good gravy, no! I never told him anything. He told me." She did, however, finally suggest that the movers were the experts in that situation.

And she endured a quarter century of short Army-ordered separations. And she endured the long, bleak years of separation during World War II. It was no easier for Mamie than for other Army wives to see her husband go off to war, even though the assignment in Europe was to be the greatest challenge of his life. She saw him only once between 1942 and 1945, years when she lost twenty-five pounds from anxiety and its accompanying insomnia.

When Ike came home after the war, he had, in Mamie's words, "changed terrifically." It may be closer to the truth that it was their relationship that had "changed terrifically." He had his own personal staff, his own routine. He was no longer dependent on Mamie for lunch money or carfare as in the prewar days. "He belonged to the world and not to me any more," Mamie told me. During the war, although Ike was a conscientious correspondent, he had been unable to share many of the details of his life. Most of the time his location and his actions were top secret. Mamie remembers that the closest he ever came to describing his location on a trip was to write, "I am someplace you would hate, way down under the ground." She learned months later that the "someplace" was Malta.

When in 1952, Ike chose a way of life that would mean permanent fame and entail constant press attention, for as he wrote in his memoirs, "Anyone who goes into politics becomes public property the day he does so," Mamie was not enthusiastic. She had never been an ambitious woman. She wanted only what was best for her husband and best did not necessarily mean the Presidency. She understood, however, that despite all the aspects of political life that she and Ike would find uncomfortable, he was swayed by those who argued that it was his duty. Duty was a concept he could not ignore, and Mamie respected him for it.

Mamie Eisenhower sums up her years in the White House with the statement, "I never pretended to be anything but Ike's wife." She did not make a career out of the Presidential years and had a detached take-it-or-leave-it attitude about life in the Executive Mansion. After years as chatelaine of the large households that were part of Ike's position as Army Chief of Staff, President of Columbia University, and Supreme Commander of NATO in Paris, she was not over-awed by one hundred and thirty-two rooms and a staff of eighty. She had led the remarkable kind of life in which she could look back and declare, "Every job Ike ever undertook was a step up." Life went on almost as if her husband had not been elected to the most influential position in the postwar world. Mamie spent a great deal of her time in the White House planning for the life she would have with Ike in

Gettysburg when they left Washington. She oversaw every detail of reconstruction and decoration for the farm they bought in 1948.

If Mamie Eisenhower were First Lady today, she would be a fish out of water, subject to pressure—which she would have resisted—to be involved in First Lady projects, to project a prescribed image. She pre-dated the era of "the press secretary to the First Lady." Her social secretary, Mary Jane McCaffrey, handled all aspects of First Lady publicity. She rarely gave interviews. They were foreign to her come-sit-on-the-couch-and-chat-with-me nature; the kind of warm communication in which by the end of five minutes you are asking her to describe each charm on her bracelet.

Mamie set foot in the Oval Office only four times during Ike's Presidency. "And each time I was in-vited," she says. It was merely the continuation of the pattern Ike and Mamie had established in their first days of marriage in their two-room apartment in San Antonio. Ike never brought his business home with him, and Mamie frankly resented it if he did. When he was home, he belonged to her world, a world of light-hearted family life where there were no pressures.

In the 1300 pages of President Eisenhower's two-volume memoirs, there are only fifty references to his wife. A detailed account of the policies and history of his administration, it reveals little of the man who set those policies and made the history, and consequently Mamie figures hardly at all. Significantly, however, Ike confirms that more than any other person Mamie bolstered his spirit and will to continue when he lay flat on his back in a Denver hospital after his first heart attack in 1955. "She was convinced," Ike wrote, "that my job as President was not yet finished."

There was only one occasion when Ike sought Mamie's guidance on a Presidential decision—whether or not to seek a second term of office. Whenever

Mamie is asked about that, she takes great care to point out that her advice was to urge Ike to do what he felt was best and to listen to his most trusted advisors. To Mamie, the White House represented the years of Ike's life that were most subject to strain and pressure. She had no sentimental attachment to the White House and often told me, "I don't miss that place at all." But she did not join her son John and her brother-in-law Milton Eisenhower in urging Ike to guard his health and not serve for four more years. "He still had a job to finish," she felt.

Everything Mamie undertook as First Lady was as Ike's wife. After his first heart attack, she signed every letter of acknowledgment and thanks for the 11,000 get-well messages, because she considered those who wrote as neighbors and friends. She entertained enthusiastically, enjoying the State Dinners and teas and all the other social duties that came with her husband's new position. Many women today view with wonder Mamie's preoccupation with perfectly planned parties and meticulous housekeeping while First Lady, but life was different then. There were long dissertations in the newspapers, for example, speculating on whether or not Mrs. Eisenhower would shake hands gloved or ungloved. Mrs. Truman and Mrs. Roosevelt had worn gloves, considering it "less fatiguing" to shake hands with them on, but Mamie, it was believed, would prefer the friendliness of the ungloved hand. (She wore gloves.) News accounts of Eisenhower era parties abounded with detailed descriptions of the ladies' dresses, the table decorations, and Mamie's costume jewelry. The fashion cry became, "If Mamie can wear junk jewelry, so can I."

Despite the seemingly fragile femininity of her two-inch-high heels and petticoated skirts, Mamie was a commanding figure within the White House. It was her home for eight years, and the staff did not make a move without consulting her first. She told me she regularly inspected every part of the house, including the coffee-break room in the basement used by the White House police, paying particular attention to the ashtrays.

She handled the financial budget—and it was often a struggle. When the Eisenhowers moved in, Mrs. Truman had left exactly $375 for redecorating. Mamie spent hours shopping for accessories that would fit the budget, including sheer curtains for the third-floor bedrooms that cost only a dollar a panel. And the staff learned to live with her major eccentricity—she could not tolerate footprints showing on the carpets before a party. Fortunately, very few of the mansion's rugs were without patterns and Mamie's favorite Bissel carpet-sweeper was not needed often. Despite her eagle eye, the staff came to love Mamie because she took such an interest in what they did and in their personal lives as well. I remember the great excitement that preceded each of Mamie's visits to her old home during my father's Presidency.

The Eisenhowers entertained more heads of state than any of their predecessors, and Mamie scrutinized every detail of the six-course State Dinners. Carnations were used on most occasions because she believed that people were not allergic to them. She delighted in dreaming up special decorations. The Easter luncheon for Senate wives in 1957 was her greatest triumph. It must have fulfilled every party fantasy Mamie ever had. Easter bunnies peeked out of robin's-egg-blue shells on the mantel of the state dining room. Butterflies of pastel net floated from the ceiling, and a birdcage was suspended from the center ring of the chandelier. The ladies wondered how two small birds could fill the room with chirps and trills until Mamie told one of the butlers to "turn down the birds."

In greeting foreign visitors, Mamie adopted the attitude that they were welcome guests in her home. When Elizabeth, the Queen Mother of Great Britain, visited Washington, my parents met her at the airport and escorted her to the White House where she would be the guest of President and Mrs. Eisenhower. Mamie warmly greeted Elizabeth as an old friend from postwar days in London. As she poured tea for Elizabeth in the West Hall sitting room, they settled down comfortably to nonstop girl talk, while my parents and Ike, who were sitting so that they could see the elevator, watched the ushers bring up trunk after trunk. My mother told me that Ike became more and more agitated as the luggage piled up. His face flushed and he rolled his eyes in disbelief as the trunks kept coming. Elizabeth and Mamie chatted on.

Creating a home for Ike was more important to Mamie than entertaining. She chose a small room on the second floor with the northern exposure painters need and turned it into a studio for Ike. It was next to the elevator so that he could slip over from the Oval Office for fifteen or twenty minutes whenever he had time. The President loved to cook and, because he could not putter around in the banquet-size kitchen in the White House without disturbing preparations for official entertaining, Mamie had a kitchen installed on the third floor, with the counters tailored to his height. Ike had done most of the cooking when they were newlyweds since, as Mamie likes to say, "I can only make two things: mayonnaise and fudge." Later on, cooking became one of his favorite ways to relieve tension. When my five-foot-three-inch sister started using the kitchen for entertaining boyfriends at the beginning of my father's administration, it was a struggle to work in "the General's kitchen," as the staff still called it. She could not reach the shelves without using a little stepladder.

Ike's health was Mamie's major concern. I remember the first time Mamie and I sat together on the second floor of the White House to watch my father address the nation. From the window we could see the brightly lighted Oval Office where technicians were testing cameras. As we waited for the speech to begin, it was unusually quiet on the second floor. No noise from behind the double doors of the family kitchen. No messages being delivered. No phone calls from the switchboard. The atmosphere of waiting and watching must have reminded Mamie of the times she had listened to Ike speak.

Mamie broke the silence. Her large blue eyes were opened wider than ever as she re-lived one of her biggest fears. "After 1955," she said, "whenever Ike gave a speech, I always sat there in utter dread that he would have a heart attack on the air." She did not need to say more for me to understand what the pressures of those last White House years must have been.

She was zealously protective of Ike. He had offered to make two campaign stops in southern Illinois for my father during the last crucial weeks of the campaign against John F. Kennedy in 1960. Two weeks before the election, however, Mamie called my mother. After Ike's last campaign trip on behalf of my father, his blood pressure had soared alarmingly. Mamie was near tears as she told my mother of her fear that if Ike tried to do too much, he would be stricken again. My father did not take the President up on his offer. On November 8, the election was decided by the closest popular vote margin in Presidential history. Kennedy carried Illinois by a mere 9,000 votes.

Although Mamie had never contemplated any role in the White House beyond that of the President's hostess and help-meet, her activities as First Lady were determined to a great degree by her health. That she accomplished as much as she did is due largely to her great determination. Ever since a bout with rheumatic fever when she was seven years old severely damaged the valves of the left side of her heart, she has been acutely conscious of each heartbeat, and has not had a high energy level. When she is fatigued or troubled, the irregular heartbeat becomes frightening in its intensity.

By the time Mamie reached the White House, she had long ago learned how to live with what doctors term a "cardiac injury." She knew how to pamper herself. Breakfast in bed and an hour or more of bed rest were part of her daily routine—despite the demands of being First Lady. And Mamie whole-heartedly believed what a skin specialist once told her—if women stayed in bed for at least one day a week, it would do more for their complexions that all the face cream in the world. Whether it is due to heredity or bed rest, at eighty, Mamie has a virtually unlined face.

She also suffers from Ménière's disease, a rare inner-ear syndrome, which was diagnosed at Walter Reed Army Hospital in 1953. The chief symptom is dizziness, and she has to hold on to someone when climbing stairs and when she is in crowds. Mamie's difficulties with her balance caused rumors that she drank heavily. Ike was so upset by the rumors about her drinking and the frequent sniping about her lack of activity that he forbade her to read *The Washington Post*. Typically, the dainty peaches-and-cream lady of iron will solved the problem by reading the *Post* secretly.

Mamie gave in to her health in only one respect. She was scared to death of flying. Ike wrote that she "never quite convinced herself that an airplane flies." But she did convince herself that her heart could not take easily altitudes over three thousand feet. Though she valiantly flew with Ike during most of his barnstorming campaign of 1953, she hated it. Characteristically, she did not try to understand or explain this fear. With a laugh and a shrug toward heaven, all she will say is, "I just don't like it."

Mamie became quite ill after a trip to the West Coast in the summer of 1971, and the doctors felt the best way to get her home to Gettysburg was by plane. My parents persuaded her to fly to Washington on board Air Force One. She agreed on the understanding that the plane would not fly much over three thousand feet. In the family sitting room on board the plane, my mother and I tried to keep Mamie diverted. We played gin rummy and chatted. Mamie was burrowed down in the large armchair by the window, her place of refuge in the treacherous air. Once in a while, she would boldy venture to peek out the window. As Air Force One soared to a cruising altitude of 32,000 feet, she remarked how beautiful the sky was from 3,000 feet. We agreed. And Mamie turned her attention back to our card game.

Considering the limitations of Mamie's physical strength, I admire the way she tried to fulfill what she felt were Ike's expectations of duty. Sadly, at the very moment when she most wanted to honor him—the state funeral in Washington—Mamie was not able to follow his casket up the forty-five steps to the rotunda of the Capitol. The small figure in black had to use the elevator.

Before Ike died, he and Mamie had decided that they would give the Gettysburg farm to the nation. Mamie had no intention of living there without Ike. She had once said, "Whenever Ike went away, the house sagged. When he came home, the house was alive again." But the only property that the Eisenhowers had ever owned in their fifty-two years of marriage was like a magnet. It drew her back. She is ambivalent about her life on the farm. She is often lonely and she is isolated from her family and most of her friends. Nor is she one to live in the past. I'm not ready to die," she often tells her son and her grandchildren. "There are too many things I want to do yet." But part of her did die with Ike. "When Ike died," Mamie told me, "the light went out of my life." And that expresses it all.

Her happiest moments are when her son and daughter-in-law or her grandchildren come to visit her. But John and Barbara Eisenhower live in Valley

Forge, Pennsylvania, a full three hours' drive from Gettysburg, and her grandchildren are even further away: David, Anne and Susan, all in New York, and Mary in Georgia. When we do go for a visit, I love to hear her voice—usually floating down from her bedroom—call out, "Sign in." The guest book in the entrance hall is a ritual at the farm and Mamie pores over it after her visitors have gone.

She is still a blithe spirit—on the surface. Widowhood has been a bitter experience in many ways. She has been hurt. Something precious has been taken from her. The public viewed Mamie as the one who had to be protected and shielded from the harshness of political life. Yet, in reality it was Mamie who watched over Ike. Now the one she protected is gone.

For more than a year after Ike's death, his bedroom remained the same—as if he had gone out for nine holes of golf and would soon return for lunch in bed and a nap. But gradually, the little room, one-third the size of the one he shared with Mamie at night has become a storage area. The scales have been pushed back into a corner. The narrow bed with the plain wooden headboard, which belonged to Mamie's grandparents, is covered with books and boxes. The personal items on his chest of drawers have been removed to make room for more books and boxes. But, despite the organized clutter, the room is still his, austere and masculine: an unframed round mirror above his bureau, the portrait he painted of David and Anne Eisenhower at the head of his bed.

He is there at every turn in the house. His gray velvet rocking chair still has the choice place in front of the television set. It has not been reupholstered, although there are bare spots on the arms where the nap has worn off. A pad by the telephone contains his handwritten phone numbers. The golf green on the lawn, now used as a sandpile for the great-grandchildren; the gone-to-seed vegetable garden; the skeet range at the end of the field in sight of Mamie's card table—all are reminders of Ike. His presence is so real that it is often painful for his grandchildren to visit the farm even now. And it is very real to Mamie. Sometimes as she lies in bed in the afternoon, she can see Ike's knobby hand, the knuckles broken so often when he was a semi-pro baseball player, grasping the railing at the top of the stairs.

Mamie needs many defenses against her memories and loneliness. She often does not come downstairs for several days at a time, but when she does come down and sit on the porch where she and Ike spent their evenings together, she fights the loneliness by playing complicated games of double-deck solitaire, while her radio or a television soap opera keeps her company. "I don't file a fingernail without turning on the radio," she likes to say. She usually wears a dressing gown from her collection of fifty, many of them more than thirty years old. When she walks, it is a slow progress. She does not move fast because of her tendency to vertigo—and also because most of her dressing gowns are trailing affairs that more than touch the ground. But the house *does* seem to sag without Ike and at twilight, Mamie retreats to her bedroom again. She has covered the emptiness of Ike's side of their king-size bed with a protective wall of books stacked four or five volumes high, boxes of stationery and greeting cards and tins of sweets. The wall stretches from head to foot.

Mamie no longer has Ike to surprise with red-and-white "lovebug" undershorts on Valentine's Day, but she continues to lavish cards and small gifts on family and friends. Propped up against several pillows in bed, she will spend four hours at a time writing the month's birthday cards. Photographs of those she remembers on special occasions, surround her. Her bureau alone holds thirty-eight. And she faithfully answers her mail from the public. Those who write announcing the birth of a child receive a "welcome to this world" letter from Mamie. She is proud of her distinctive, bold handwriting, and each message is a work of art. She pays a great deal of attention to it and is distressed when it is not perfect. "I can't seem to get my M's right today," she told me once when I visited her at the farm.

Mamie tries valiantly not to be a possessive matriarch. Often we do not learn until it is too late how much she has counted on a visit or a phone call that never came. Mamie has seen five of the seven apartments David and I have lived in since our marriage, but in her effort not to cling, she has never spent the night. I understand why she made the trips to visit us in Virginia Beach and even in Atlanta Beach, Florida. She wanted to be able to visualize the rooms. "I sit up here in bed and think about you in your nest," she tells me. And whenever we talk on the telephone, her first question is "Where are you?" And I tell her that I am in the kitchen or the bedroom and know she is picturing it all in her mind.

She believes in family obligations and loyalty and uses her telephone as a link with those she loves. Every other Sunday (she alternates with "Mike" Moore) she calls her Uncle Joel Carlson, now in his nineties, in Boone, Iowa, where he was born and where he has lived all his life. When Uncle Joel and Mamie spent Thanksgiving with my family in the White House in 1969, we discovered that Joel was not a docile character. He never was. When Mamie was born, Uncle Joel's first comment upon seeing the four-pound infant was that she looked like "a little picked chicken." During the Washington visit, Joel followed his own rigid schedule. Since Mamie was also accustomed to having schedules built around her wishes, there was a barely submerged conflict, although Mamie asked us to try to follow Joel's routine. It included a Coke at ten (Mamie has hers at eleven), dinner at six (Mamie usually dines at seven-thirty), bed at eight-thirty (Mamie retires two hours later).

A typical incident was the family movie party. We had a six o'clock dinner for Uncle Joel's sake and planned to watch a film afterward. In the theater, Joel settled into his chair, and promptly fell asleep. At precisely eight o'clock, the alarm clock inside Uncle Joel's head went off. He woke up, rose from his chair and announced, "Well, it's my bedtime. Goodnight." Somehow the spell of the movie was broken when Uncle Joel's silhouette loomed on the screen as he slowly sauntered out. It was touching to see Mamie submit to orders from "Uncle," and slightly unnerving to hear him scold his seventy-three-year-old niece, who was as spunky and saucy as when Ike first met her on the parade ground at Fort Sam Houston so many years before.

Mamie rather enjoys racy novels. "To think—at my age—learning all about phonography," she says, taking pleasure in her conscious mispronunciation of the word. And she is a past master of the pointed remark. When I called her one Sunday, which happened to be Father's Day, she said, "Tell that beau of yours I'm sorry I couldn't send him a Father's Day card this year." It was a not-so-subtle expression of her desire for a fourth generation Eisenhower in the male line of the family. Her relations with family members are not always placid, but the disagreements are nothing more than skirmishes. Mamie says what she thinks and that is the end of the argument. She rarely sulks or holds grudges.

Because harboring hostility toward others is not part of her own personality, Mamie cannot understand it when she meets it in other people—and closes her eyes to it. If she reads something ugly about someone she cares for, she shrugs, "Oh, I don't believe that." Despite President Truman's belittlement of Ike in *Plain Speaking*, Mamie does not express any emotion other than puzzlement. In the tone of someone who is disappointed in a child she says, "Mr. Truman knew better." She prefers to focus on the happier aspects of the Truman-Eisenhower relationship, such as her Spanish lessons with Mrs. Truman. During the Truman Administration, a group of women met at the White House once a week for lessons and a luncheon. They rotated the shopping, cooking and serving duties. Did she learn any Spanish? "Heavens, no! We just talked."

Although Mamie loves to gossip in the sense of old-fashioned girl talk, she does not indulge in dissecting famous personalties. She is tight-lipped even about those she knew well, like General Douglas MacArthur. The most she has ever divulged about the seven years Ike served as MacArthur's aide in the Philippines is that the General was charming to women—and that he rouged his cheeks.

The woman who has met or entertained most of the great figures of the twentieth century is simply incapable of name dropping. Her idea of fun is well suited to the pace of life in Gettysburg. She turns down embassy and government invitations and finds more fascination in discovering the latest junk food in the grocery stores. She is always coming home with new things to try. She can tell you the most recent sugar prices and whether eggs are "as high as a cat's back." Thirty years of making ends meet on an Army salary have made Mamie vigilant about saving. Even today, despite the money earned by Ike's best seller, *Crusade in Europe*, Mamie watches every penny. And scrutinizes every bill, particularly the electric bills. One does not waste electricity in Mamie's house. Not long ago, a visiting family member could not sleep, so he decided to get up and read. Instead of ruining his eyes on the dimly lighted porch, he spent several hours reading in the hall bathroom. But he made one mistake. The next morning, Mamie's first order of business was to find out who had forgotten to turn off the light in the bathroom!

When Ike died, he left a huge wardrobe of suits. Mamie could not bear to see them go to waste, so I went through them and picked out five or six for David. Mamie was visiting us in the White House at the time and we arranged to have the tailor come when David got home from a golf game one afternoon. David dislikes shopping and dislikes having clothes fitted even more, but when he got home that day he could not escape our carefully laid trap. Mamie was ensconced on the blue sofa in the third-floor study with her cigarette case and ashtray next to her, and the tailor was there with the measuring tape around his neck and a big pincushion on his wrist. For the next hour and a half, David had to stand still while his grandfather's suits were being fitted to him. To this day, when Mamie is extolling my virtues to her friends, she willl say, "Julie is so saving. She had Ike's suits remade for David." David is still wearing those suits today. They were very good suits.

Mamie is never happier than when I compliment her on a dress and she can say she bought it at Penney's for twelve dollars. She always pronounces the store's name as *Penné* with a mock French accent. It is Mamie's gentle way of spoofing those women who devote time and money to being the first to wear the latest high-fashion designer clothes. There is nothing pretentious about the farm, either. One is aware of this in the first few minutes. In the entrance hall, Mamie has two objects of equal value to her on display—a four-dollar ceramic elephant dressed in an Uncle Sam suit and an antique bronze-doré French clock.

Mamie is simply herself and she accepts others for what they are. She is intolerant only of those who "put on airs." Perhaps it is her Army background that makes her wary of social climbing and of those who pull rank. She is proud of Ike's cow-town origins. I once heard a cultured woman from New York, whose family sets great store by its social register status, tell Mamie the involved story of how her ancestors were among the early arrivals in the country and their great importance in the Colonial government, ad infinitum up to the Seventies. Mamie listened politely and then she chuckled, "Oh, yes, I know all about that. The Douds came over from Sweden in 1600." Since there were no Swedes in America in 1600, let alone Douds, her companion could hardly miss the point.

Part of Mamie's charm is that along with her unpretentiousness, she frequently enjoys being the center of attention. Because she has an engaging personality —she is fun, a flirt, one amusing contradiction after another—people have always been attracted to Mamie. And as Ike rose in the Army hierarchy, more and more people paid court to her. Yet she is blissfully unaware that she enjoys special attention. She likes to tell stories that illustrate just how much a part of the mainstream she really is. Her favorite is about spending Easter with us at Camp David. The Navy stewards dyed eggs with the names of each family member to serve as place cards at breakfast on Easter Day. Mamie relates that the eggs all bore formal titles —"The President," "Mrs. Nixon," but hers, to her delight, read just "Mamie."

I saw these two facets of Mamie's personality—on one hand desire for the simple life, on the other the focus of attention—during a jaunt to some of Gettysburg's tourist attractions. At the Electric Map, President Lincoln's Train, and the Wax Museum, Mamie was greeted excitedly by the managers and special tours were arranged for us. She enjoyed the recognition and would have been hurt if it had not been forthcoming. Yet we concluded our royal progress in a crowded Hardee's, nonchalantly eating hamburgers.

Mamie's attitude toward Secret Service protection is that those who claim they did not like it (i.e., granddaughter-in-law Julie) are pretending. "Everyone likes a little special attention." For a young person, however, being guarded is a nightmare. It means a complete lack of freedom to go anywhere or see anyone without a shadow. Former First Ladies are entitled to Secret Service protection until their death or remarriage. Mamie's agents are an important part of her life now. Without them, she could not travel as she does. And they are her friends. When she makes plans for the holidays, one of her major concerns is how they will affect the agents with small children. Ever since her first days in the White House, she has known each man personally, whether or not he enjoyed flying, liked fudge, how many children he had.

When she speaks of the agents to friends she calls them "my boys." They are held dear for different reasons. One is a survivor of David's childhood summers at camp, of the rattlesnakes in the showers and of the terrible food. Another, of impressive proportions, is affectionately referred to as "Twinkletoes." He breezes in to visit with Mamie, light on his feet despite his bulk, and lighter still in his comments. These men whose job it is to protect her have softened the devastating changes of widowhood. Yet even these friendships are susceptible to change. The agents serve on orders from the Department of the Treasury and at any moment they can be, and are, transferred. Mamie's family is still her center of gravity as it has been all her life.

Mamie Doud Eisenhower is the most sentimental woman I have ever known. Not long ago at the farm, I opened a drawer and found an old piece of paper folded into quarters. Tucked inside was a tooth, the string still attached. In pencil, John Eisenhower had written, "Dear fairy, please leave my tooth."

And she still believes in young love. It was Mamie who viewed the romance of her eighteen-year-old grandson with unabashed sentimentality and unquestioning acceptance. She grew starry-eyed when she talked to Ike about our college courtship. Ike, on the other hand, wrote David a freshman year "now that you are a college man" letter in which he outlined a plan for the future that, if the various educational degrees he suggested were earned, allowed for marriage when David was around thirty-three. When we were married our junior year in college, I wore the delicately thin garter of blue silk and lace Mamie had worn fifty-two years before. And on my finger was her mother's engagement ring.

Mamie cannot remember the date of the Geneva Summit meeting, but more than sixty years after she first set eyes on Dwight David Eisenhower she recalls every detail of their meeting down to the Sunday afternoon outfit she wore. Mamie must have been a vision in a pink cretonne skirt with an embroidered silk crêpe de chine blouse, a wide cummerbund with pink roses, and tiny rose-shaped coral earrings. The costume was completed by a chipped straw hat with a wide band of the same material as the cummerbund. Meeting Ike was the most significant event of her life.

Mamie lived for one man, and that man was dominated by the concept of service to his country. But she was not steam-rollered by his career or caught up in his crusades. Her concept of service was much narrower. She is a woman of tremendous self-confidence, a strong character who has obtained almost everything she wanted from life. It suited her to serve Ike because she loved him and admired him until he died in 1969. To most, ideal love is not belonging to someone, but it was for Mamie. She was Ike's wife, pure and simple, and happy about it.

Mamie Eisenhower has no interest in the immortality syndrome. She seems unconcerned about memorials to her husband or the necessity of reminding people of what he accomplished. She has a simple faith that what Ike was will shine through. What he was to her and to himself is what truly counts. When Ike was buried in Abilene, Dean Miller, the pastor of the church in Palm Desert where Ike and Mamie used to spend winters, captured the essence of Mamie Eisenhower's life: "Mrs. Eisenhower graciously shared her husband with the world, but he belonged uniquely to her."